COME ON, CHORISTERS!

A History

of

The Chorister School, Durham

Brian Crosby

ISBN 0-9537524-1-0

First edition 1999
Revised and extended edition 2008

Published by Brian Crosby and printed in Great Britain
by Prontaprint, Durham

Cover photograph: AirFotos, Newcastle
(copyright: Prontaprint, Durham)

CONTENTS

Foreword to the present edition

I knew when I was appointed as Head here in March 2002 I was taking a step into history. When Dr Crosby gave me his book, *Come on, Choristers!*, which I read on my summer holidays, I became much more aware that I was not just a Head but the present custodian of a very precious thing, a living tradition which had a rich, full and very long past, a thriving present and a future for which I was in large part in charge. It was a terrifying way to start a new appointment.

Now as I write this I am into my seventh year. A generation of choristers has come and gone. Time has flown by very quickly, and I am now able to join in the celebration of the school's Diamond Jubilee as a prep school, 60 years since 1948 and the first non-chorister day pupils and boarders.

Dr Crosby is still a regular part of the school's life and not just its past. He asked me to write a foreword for the new edition of his book, which I am delighted to do. I am very happy that he is still recording the significant events of the history of this special place.

In this jubilee year we have just opened a new Nursery, and in September 2009 we will see the historic entry into the Cathedral Choir of a top line of girls.

It is an exciting time to be Head, seeing an exciting present become history, hopefully securing the future for many more years to come.

Ian Hawksby
Durham, 2008

Preface to the present edition

A new edition of *Come on, Choristers!* affords the opportunity not only to add the latest chapters of an on-going story, but to re-assess what has been said about the origins of the school, and to make use of the further archival material which has become available. Nevertheless, because over 90% of the old text has been incorporated, it is felt that the old title, which extends the encouragement voiced on the games field to the school as it journeys through the centuries, should be retained.

In terms of presentation, quotations excepted, two changes have been implemented. 'Quire' is now used of the location in the cathedral, and 'choir' of the singers; and following the example of the plaque in the south Quire aisle, which lists the Masters of the Choristers since 1541, surnames are now rendered as the individuals themselves usually did. There are, of course, some for whom no signatures have survived, and others who were far from consistent. For them frequency of occurrence in the records has usually been the determining factor.

A word of warning needs to be given to those who have become familiar with cathedral hierarchies only since 2000, when Durham adopted the 1999 *Cathedrals Measure*. The change then of the name of the governing body from the Dean & Chapter to the Chapter scarcely affects the understanding of this book, unlike the change in 2002 of the meaning of the word 'precentor'. It is now used of one of the major clergy, but between 1541 and 2002 it was applied to the minor canon who was responsible for the choir and its music. This book is careful to use the title appropriate to the time.

Finally, I must express my gratitude to Raymond Lawrence, Stephen Drew and Ian Hawksby for their willingness to discuss what I proposed writing about their regimes; to James Lancelot, the Master of the Choristers since 1985, for his opinions about the changing role and routine of the choristers; to the Chapter of Durham Cathedral for the access I have been given to its archives and for permission to include certain illustrations; to the staff of Archives & Special Collections, Durham University Library, for fielding my many queries; and to Joan Williams, Assistant Librarian at The Cathedral Library, for her general help and in particular for scrutinizing the proofs.

Brian Crosby
Durham, 2008

Foreword to the first edition

My appointment to be Headmaster of The Chorister School in 1994 was marked by various presents from Dr Crosby. One was a copy of *Dobsons Drie Bobbes*, another was a copy of Canon Ganderton's Speech Day Addresses and yet another was a copy of Dr Crosby's own monograph *Choristers and their Masters*. I was, that is to say, aware from the first that I was joining a school with a long tradition and a rich history – and its own distinguished historian.

Dr Crosby has given a great deal of time since his retirement from the school in 1996 to the rewriting and expanding and bringing up to date of his earlier work. It used mischievously to be suggested that he was probably teaching at The Chorister School when Queen Boadicea was a lass. Although his own memory does not extend quite that far, his meticulous researches over many years take us informatively and vividly into the circumstances of the school's emergence at the beginning of the fifteenth century and its subsequent development, while his personal recollections and discussions with former pupils and teachers give his presentation of its recent history an agreeably anecdotal vigour. It is our great good fortune that our school's story has such a teller; it is a story that will interest all the school's former pupils, parents and friends, and indeed all who are interested in school, Cathedral or choir.

Dr Crosby is giving all the profits from the sale of his book to the school, and I am grateful to him for such generosity. His still greater gift to the school will remain this authoritative and affectionate chronicle of a place which he loves and to which he has devoted his whole career. It is, evidently, that kind of a place; and those of us involved with its continuing story must hope that succeeding episodes will find as enthusiastic a historian in its times to come.

Stephen Drew
Durham, 1999

Preface to the first edition

Durham Cathedral: Choristers and their Masters, published in 1980, tried to unfold to those interested in cathedral music something of Durham's choral tradition, and it tried to tell those associated with The Chorister School something of the school's history over the centuries. For the latter group there was also an appendix in which the Revd Canon John Grove gave a personal account of his twenty-one years as Headmaster (1957-78). The overall result was unsatisfactory, for neither group was given as much information as it might have been, and the style adopted was also something of a compromise. In view of this, it has been decided to produce two separate books, even though, with the organists also the choristers' only masters for over 350 years, there will be some repetition of facts. This book deals with the history of the school.

Although the framework of *Choristers and their Masters* has been retained, all its text has been examined and much of it revised. Far more has come to light about the period from 1876 to 1957, and the author has now included his own assessment of 1957 onwards. Finally, every attempt has been made to flesh out the historical 'dry bones' with information about the boys, their masters and the routine.

Quotations from documents in Latin have been translated. With other quotations superscript letters have been lowered and contractions expanded, but the original spelling has been preserved. Editorial suggestions have been enclosed in square brackets. Dates before 1752, and the spelling of surnames, have been rendered to conform with modern usage.

My thanks go to Mr Drew, the Headmaster, for encouraging me to revise and update the previous booklet; to the Dean & Chapter, for allowing me access to its muniments and for permission to include certain illustrations; to those veritable mines of information, Alan Piper, Pat Mussett and Roger Norris, for their help over many years; to certain proof-readers who wish to remain anonymous; and to those former members of the school, who wittingly or unwittingly have provided me with information.

Brian Crosby
Durham, 1999

The author (a self-portrait)

Little did I think, when as student I threw tennis balls back from the South Bailey into the school yard (the school was then in 4-5 The College) that I would shortly embark upon a long-term association with the school.

According to records, I started teaching at the school in September 1957, at the same time as John Grove became Headmaster. However, when I remarked in the 1980s to a former pupil, who had left in July 1957, that we had just missed each other, he replied that this was not so, that he remembered me helping with games on Saturday evenings during his last term. He was not mistaken, for I did indeed help then. My involvement was at the invitation of Canon Ganderton, the retiring Headmaster, who had interviewed me on behalf of John Grove. As a result I was not a completely fresh face in the September, for I was already known to many of the staff and to some of the boys and their parents.

Over the years I gained in knowledge about the history of the cathedral, the school, and the choir and its music. Apparently, I must have spoken with some authority, for boys (and staff) started suggesting, not only that I remembered the cathedral being built, but that my antiquity was even greater. In one Maths lesson I inadvertently gave support to these rumours. In my enthusings about the numbers in Pythagorean triads I meant to say "I have always been fascinated by Pythagoras, ever since I first met it at school". Unfortunately, the word "him" came out instead of "it"! The boys must have been listening, for there was an immediate eruption of laughter. This prompted me to have the verbal equivalent of an 'action-replay'. Stopping a few words short of the slip of the tongue I queried, "I didn't say that, did I?" In chorus the class replied, "Oh yes, you did!" After the lesson a boarder quietly asked, "Please sir, was that as a fellow-pupil or teacher?"

Teaching can be rewarding in many ways. I have derived great pleasure in sharing in the achievements of children of all abilities. A scholar gaining a top scholarship, a not so able child grasping a point in a lesson, a young chorister's first short solo, a music exam success, taking part in a concert or music competition, having a part in a School Play, a handicapped child gaining a '1-Star' at athletics, being selected for a school team, being appointed to a position of responsibility, a kind act towards another child – all these things have brought equal delight. Rewarding too has been the rapport with children, their trust, and being able to reassure them when in my later years they came to me at all times of day and night with their problems. I count myself fortunate to have spent my entire career in such a happy school set in incomparable surroundings.

1. The historical setting

The present structure of the school

The Chorister School, Durham, is today in many ways a typical preparatory school. It accepts fee-paying boarders and day pupils, both boys and girls. Its aim is to give those pupils every opportunity to develop their academic, sporting and artistic talents, and also their social skills. Where it differs from most of the others is that it has also a group of pupils whose fees are partly funded by a cathedral authority in return for the musical contribution they make at some of the cathedral services.

Relatively small though this group of choristers is, it is the core of The Chorister School and it has given the school its present name. Indeed, from its beginnings centuries ago right up to 1948 the choristers were, with just a few exceptions,[1] the school's only pupils. In accepting eight other boarders and four day boys in September that year Canon Ganderton saw fulfilled an aspiration he had implied in his first Speech Day Report in January 1930. What finally brought about the expansion were the findings of Inspectors following the 1944 Education Act. They too felt that on social and academic grounds a school of just 24 choristers, with a Headmaster and one assistant master, was too small.

Identifying origins

It has been mentioned that the choristers have part of their fees paid for them in return for their musical contribution at services. This situation can be traced back through several centuries. As one probes backwards it transpires that it was only in about 1906 that it was decided that all future choristers should be boarders, and that from 1541 to 1856 they had only been ten in number. 1541 was when, following the dissolution of the monasteries by Henry VIII, what had been the monastic priory-cathedral of Durham was re-constituted a cathedral only, and it is when the Dean & Chapter came into being. But 1541 is not when the school began. It existed in monastic times, for among the monastic muniments are copies of the contracts drawn up from 1430 onwards with the professional musicians who were appointed to instruct a group of eight boys in the art of music.

---

[1] For information about one of the exceptions see pp. 82-4.

Where the problem lies is in determining just how far back into the monastic period one should go. Any attempt to identify the boys with the novices who were taught in the western aisle of the cloisters, and to go back not just to 995, when the community of St Cuthbert first arrived in Durham, but to Lindisfarne, must be rejected as an over-zealous seeking after antiquity. The novices were training to be monks, they were not an extra group introduced to sing at some of the services.

To be considered more seriously is the almonry school. This type of school can be traced back to the early fourteenth century, for at some point between 1301 and 1309 the Canterbury provincial chapter passed a statute requiring its monasteries to provide boys capable of serving at private masses.[2] This edict re-introduced to the monasteries the younger generation which had been lost when the Lateran Council of 1215 banned the practice of child oblation, of parents handing over young children to the care of the monasteries.[3] Although the Canterbury requirement was not extended to the northern province until 1343, the development may have reached Durham earlier, for in 1333 Richard de Bury became Bishop of Durham. Hard on his appointment are payments of 6s. 8d, "to the boys of the chapel of the Lord Bishop of Durham" and "to a clerk of the Bishop, the master of the boys".[4] As these payments do not recur the inference is that the monastery took steps to provide its own resources.

Durham's school was associated not with the almonry which attended to the needs of ill and elderly monks, but with a second one which catered for a number of elderly men and women. Many of these may have formerly been employed by the monastery or been members of their families or related to the monks. This second almonry was located on the east side of the North Bailey slightly to the north of the gateway to the precincts.[5] Precisely when it was adapted to include a school cannot be determined, but in view of the payments mentioned above it may be significant that in 1338 £13. 10s. 0d.

---

[2] R. Bowers, "Choral Institutions within the English Church:- their constitution and development 1340-1500" (Ph.D. thesis, Univ. of East Anglia; 1975), 4086.

[3] Dom D. Knowles, *The Religious Orders in England*, 3 vols (1948-59), ii, 294.

[4] J. T. Fowler (ed.), *Extracts from the Account Rolls of the Abbey of Durham*, 3 vols (Surtees Society, xcix, c, ciii; 1898-1901), ii, 527 (for 1335-6) and 530 (1336-7). The translations from the original Latin given here and elsewhere are my own. The dates are given thus because the accounts covered part of each year. The Chapter archives are in the care of Archives & Special Collections, Durham University Library, at 5 The College. This building housed at least some of the school from 1906 to 1970.

[5] *Rolls*, i, 200-2. The almonry may have been on the site of 24-6 North Bailey.

was set aside "on the repair of the middle of the Infirmary outside the gate". About the school the author of *Rites* has this to say:

> Ther weare certaine poor children onely maynteyned and releyved with ye almesse & Benevolence of the whole house, which weare called ye childrine of ye aumerey going daily to ye fermery schole being all together mayntened by ye whole Co[n]vent with meate drynke and lerni'ge.[6]

As with the elderly men and women it is likely that many of the children already had some connection with the monastery. They were "poor" only in the sense that had there not been that association they were unlikely to have received an education. Yes, the monastery was a caring employer, but it was also providing itself with potential future monks and lay employees.

The first reference to the boys occurs in 1347-8 with the payment, "to the boy bishop of the almonry, 3s. 4d."; and similar payments are found regularly in the financial accounts of the monastery and its dependent cells through to 1537-8. Payments to their master are first mentioned in 1351-2.[7]

Durham, like many other places, had a Boy Bishop who presided over the festivities associated with St Nicholas and with Holy Innocents' Day (28 December), when the boys dressed up as their seniors and behaved as if they were them. Because at Salisbury, a non-monastic cathedral, detailed financial records and even some of the sermons delivered by the Boy Bishop have been preserved,[8] it is disappointing that nothing is known about the nature of the Durham celebrations. However, it must be remembered that at Durham such activities were but minor items in the life and records of the monastery.

The almonry boys, however, are not to be thought of as a group playing a single role at particular services, but as individuals simultaneously

---

[6] J. T. Fowler (ed.), *Rites of Durham* (Sur. Soc., cvii; 1903), 91. *Rites*, written c.1593, is best described as the recollections of one who had been associated with the monastic community at the time of the Dissolution.

[7] Lytham roll, and *Rolls*, ii, 483. I am indebted to Mr John McKinnell for the Lytham reference. Because "wars at that time" resulted in the cancellation of the celebrations in 1405, and winter was not the normal 'battle season', Mr McKinnell has suggested that the Durham festivities may have taken place much earlier in the year, possibly just before Pentecost.

[8] D. H. Robertson, *Sarum Close* (1938), 78-94. In May 1998 a Durham Boy Bishop pageant devised by Mr McKinnell was enacted by pupils from Bow School, St Margaret's School and The Chorister School. The schools with their Bishop processed along the banks from Prebends' Bridge to St Oswald's church where the young Bishop warned his listeners that devotion to cars was resulting in a legless generation.

assisting a number of priests at different altars. Their role could have included some singing. As time progressed an occasional collective role may have emerged, and this may have included making a positive contribution to the choral side of worship.

One of the services they could in due course have attended as a group was the Mass held in honour of the Virgin Mary. This was celebrated in the Galilee Chapel (Durham's Lady Chapel). The Lady Mass was not part of the monastic offices because its focal point was not the offering up of praise to God. Because its structure and musical content were not governed by traditions evolved over centuries it afforded the opportunity to introduce the developments which were taking place in the sphere of music. This led to the realization that the musical impact would be greater if a possibly smaller group were specially trained by a skilled musician (known as the Cantor). What needs determining is when this realization bore fruit.

Immediately, a false trail has to be rejected. It is incorrect to conclude that a complaint about a lack of suitable secular (*i.e.*, non-monk) voices at Durham had anything to do with those being taught by such an instructor. The criticism was made by members of the monastery of St Mary's, York, when they conducted a Visitation of the monastery on behalf of the Benedictine Order in probably 1384. Included in their report is:

> It is found that there were wont to be clerks singing organum and assisting the monks in the song which is called trebill, and they are no longer there, to the great inconvenience and frustration of the brothers singing in the Quire.[9]

It is the word 'trebill' which is misleading, for it refers not to the pitch of one of the parts but to the highest voice in three-part polyphony. The 'clerks' whose absence was affecting that polyphony were adult singers. Their presence in Durham has been traced back to 1356-7.[10]

The 1380s also hold the earliest payments to the Cantor, a secular musical expert. Money is allocated to him between 1382 and 1386, in 1386-7 there is "to the Cantor at Christmas", and in 1387-8 "to Nicholas the

---

[9] W. A. Pantin (ed.), *Chapters of the English Black Monks, 1215-1540*, iii (Camden 3rd Series, liv; 1937), 83-4. Through his knowledge of the number of monks at Durham at different dates Mr Alan Piper (formerly of Archives & Special Collections, Durham University Library) has been able to determine the date of this Visitation.

[10] Chamberlain's roll. There are many references to this group in the account rolls of the monastery and its dependent cells.

Cantor".[11] Then on 10 June [13]90 one of recommendations made to Prior Robert [Berrington of] Walworth (1374-91) proposed:

> Item, as much as for [enhancing] the dignity of divine worship [as for] inspiring the devotion of the people let both musical harmony and [ceremonial] be had in the Quire in accordance with ancient custom. Chiefly on solemn feast days and at other times on Saturdays at festal masses of St Mary, which however as ... let a suitable Cantor-Instructor who knows how to teach the you[ths to sing] be ... at the expense of the house.
>
> Response: Let this article be rectified.[12]

Some of the matter included in the passage is of considerable moment. With Berrington agreeing that the points raised should be rectified much of its content is not innovatory but "in accordance with ancient custom". The passage shows that for some time harmony had enhanced the musical offering on major feast days and that the cult of Blessed Mary the Virgin was flourishing and being celebrated with a weekly festal mass. It appears that these services were attended by members of the public and that youths were already contributing vocally.

But the hopes that this recommendation of 1390 marks the introduction of the Cantor-Instructor and a group of young singers find little support during the next twenty-five years. There are only three payments to the former, and they fall within a three-year period. That in 1395-6, "to the Informator of the boys for his salary" seems clear enough, but those in 1396-7 and 1397-8 "to the Cantor"[13] could relate to his other duties. As for the younger generation, one has to wait until 1414-15 for a payment to them.[14]

Also falling within the year 1414-15 was the granting in June 1414 of the Licence founding the Langley chantry. As well as requiring the two chantry priests to offer up prayers and masses for the souls of Langley's parents – and in due course for that of the Bishop himself – the Licence stipulated that:

---

[11] Bursar's Book 'D' and two Hostiller's rolls (for the second see also *Rolls*, i, 134). The earlier fourteenth-century *Repertorium* confirms that the position had been provided for financially by 1345.

[12] Locellus XXVII, no.35, Item 2. The dots indicate where text has been lost and reconstruction is not possible.

[13] The Almoner's roll, Bursar's Book 'E' and the Hostiller's roll, respectively.

[14] *Rolls*, ii, 300 suggests that the Terrar made a payment in 1401-2, but that roll has now been dated 1421-2.

the chaplains shall be sufficiently instructed and shall keep schools, one in grammar and the other in song, in the city of Durham in places to be assigned ... teaching poor persons *gratis* and receiving moderate stipends from those who are willing to pay, and the chaplain keeping the school in song shall be bound to be present and sing at the mass of St Mary with chant in the church of Durham or the said chapel with any of his scholars in competent number, but the one governing the grammar school need only be present on Sundays and double feasts ...[15]

Until the 1960s it was widely assumed that just as Durham School was the successor of the Langley grammar school,[16] so The Chorister School was descended directly from his song school. But where Langley's city grammar school and the monastery's almonry grammar school had much in common, and were merged in 1541, the song schools followed very different courses.[17] Both song schools survived the dissolution of the monastery, the Langley one's purpose having no musical associations but being to prepare children for the grammar school.[18]

Key to the Plan, opposite

1. *St Cuthbert's shrine*
2. *Organ over Quire door*
3. *Jesus Altar*
4. *Nave organ*
5. *Altar of BVM and Langley chantry*
6. *Novices' school*
7. *Site of the almonry and its school*
8. *Site of monastic song school*
9. *Dean & Chapter song school, 1541-1633*
10. *Song school, 1633+*
11. *Song school, 1661-c.1899*
12. *Present site of song school (over)*
13. *D & C grammar school, 1661-1843*
14. *Site of revestry*
15. *St Mary's College, 1919-52*

House numbers (current) in The College are indicated by Roman numerals

---

[15] *Calendar of Patent Rolls, Henry V: 1413-16*, 206 *et seq*.

[16] This is confirmed by the deed dated 31 May 1541 (3.3.Pont.10) whereby Bishop Cuthbert Tunstall handed over the Bishop's schools to the Dean & Chapter.

[17] 'Song school' denoted a location as well as a tier of education. In terms of the former, the meaning has narrowed. Until the late nineteenth century it described the place where the choristers received their entire education. Now it is reserved for the room in which they practise some of the music they are to sing.

[18] So the appointment of John Rangell in 1582 (Hunter MS 13, f. 49^r, in the Cathedral Library) and other later appointments.

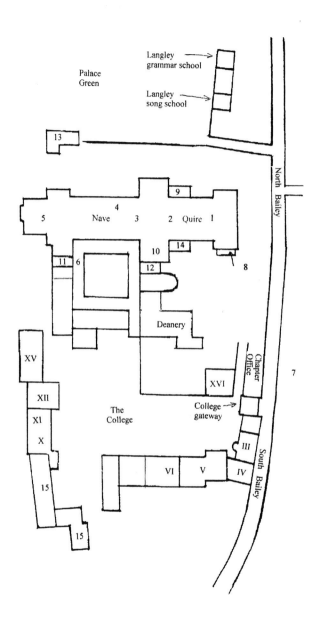

Plan of the cathedral and its environs

This it continued to do until *c*.1690. But even in monastic times the schools were quite distinct. Their separate identities have been established by a consideration of their sites, the names of their masters, the sources of the stipends and the fact that the Langley masters could charge fees from those who could afford them.[19] Moreover, the number of Langley chantry chaplains reduced to one in 1419. When the second was re-introduced in 1438, some years after a five-year renovation of the Galilee chapel and Langley's death, the whole situation was reviewed by the monastery. The almonry school and the grammar school were combined under the chaplain teaching grammar. This merger quickly proved unsatisfactory, and the schools resumed their separate existences in 1442. As for the song school chaplain, he was required to be present at Mass and Vespers in the Quire, but his scholars and the Lady Mass in the Galilee Chapel were not even mentioned.

Nevertheless, in spite of all these points, or because of them, the feeling persists that, different though his song school may have been, the founding of the Langley chantry may have served to accelerate the steps taken by the monastery.

---

[19] B. Crosby, "The Song School at Durham", *Durham University Journal* (1968), 63-72.

2. The Monastic Period

1414-30: First steps

Although the petition for a Cantor-Instructor had been aired and approved in 1390, it was not until 1414-15, over twenty years later, that the younger generation begins to be mentioned. The two payments that year, the first by the Sacrist of 16s. 6d. "for five surplices made for the boys serving at private masses",[1] and the second of 20s. by the Terrar, "for garments for the clerks of the church", probably relate to the same purchase, for the Terrar made his payment to the Sacrist. Similar payments then occur in the rolls of one or other of the two officials through to 1421-2 and beyond, the recipients being described as "little clerks" and "boys of the church". Somewhat different and caring is the payment in 1416 by the Bursar of 12d. "to divers boys enjoying themselves in the presence of the same Prior this year at the feast of St Stephen [26 December]".[2]

Running parallel, and beginning in 1415-16, is a series of other payments. These relate to the instruction, and to the adults who gave it. It was given in the first year not by a secular employee but by one of the senior monks:[3]

> To Dom William Kyblesworth for instructing the novices, 3s. 4d.
> To Dom W. Kibblesworth for teaching the young monks, 5s.
> To Dom William Kyblesworth for instructing the youths, 3s. 4d.
> To William Kyblesworth on the authority of the Lord [Prior], 2s.[4]

That the recipients are described as 'novices', 'young monks' and 'youths' may not point so much to three different groups as to a new initiative, and uncertainty on the part of the funding obedientiaries about the recipients. This uncertainty may also account for the lack of information about the nature of the instruction. It is a pity that the reason for the fourth payment is not known, for in the same place in the roll for 1414-15 is a payment of 3s. 4d. to Dom Robert Masham on the same authority.

---

[1] *Rolls*, ii, 405; and ii, 301 for that by the Terrar. Five was the usual number.
[2] *Ibid.*, iii, 614.
[3] Kibblesworth's association with the priory began in *c*.1387. He went up to Durham College, Oxford, in 1390-1, finally returning to Durham in 1410-11.
[4] The payments are by the Almoner, Hostiller, Sacrist and Feretrar. For the second and third see, *Rolls*, i, 139 and ii, 406.

In 1416-17, the period during which John Wessington became Prior and Kibblesworth died, the earlier uncertainties disappear and the payments become more specific in their detail:

To William Chantour for the instruction of the youths in singing, 7s.
To the Cantor for instructing the youths in polyphony, 2s. 2d.
To the master of the polyphonists, 2s. 6d.
To paying William Chantour what had been formally agreed, 10s.
To the Cantor for instructing the youths, 5s.[5]

The aptly named Chantour was not a monk. Neither was his successor, Richard Wymond (1418-22), who was paid for instructing youths, monks and also "his colleagues". Like Chantour he was paid "according to the formal agreement". This explains why he himself sang at unspecified services in the Quire, and why he was provided with a summer garment. It may be felt that 'youths' describes an older age group than 'boys', but what is important is that there was a secular group being instructed in singing and that someone was being paid for teaching them.

After Wymond came Hugh Westmoreland (1423-4) and William Davy (1424-6). As Wymond and Westmoreland had brothers who were monks[6] it is not inconceivable that they had gained their musical proficiency as 'choristers'. Like Kibblesworth and Chantour, Wymond received payment for instructing various groups; like Chantour he was paid "according to the formal agreement". Westmoreland and Davy, too, may have had some sort of contract – they were paid in full by the Hostiller.

Dating from the time of these early Cantors is a Durham Processional. Its rubric for Palm Sunday affords proof of the use of boys' voices. It states, "the boys in a high place sing the antiphon, *Glory, laud, and honour*".[7] The "high place" may have been an organ loft, it may have been the triforium or even higher.

1430-87: The contracts with John Stele

Some of his predecessors may have had formal agreements, but that drawn up on 22 December 1430 with John Stele is the earliest for which a copy survives. By it, Stele, who may have acquired his musical skills as one of the

---

5   *Rolls*, i, 226 and ii, 287, 462 and 406, and the Sacrist's roll. Chantour also received 6d. from the Almoner in 1420-1 for an unspecified reason.
6   John Wymond was a monk from 1414 to 1423-4, and Robert Westmoreland from 1424 to 1447. Richard Wymond later became a monk, but not at Durham.
7   British Library, Royal MS 7.A.VI, f. 118.

early choristers,[8] agreed to serve the Prior and Convent for the rest of his life. As Cantor, Stele was to instruct to the best of his ability eight secular boys and an unspecified number of monks in the whole art of music. This was deemed to consist of instruction in playing the organ; and, in the sphere of singing, in coping with "Pryktenote, Faburdon, Deschaunte, and counter". Although he was not a monk, Stele was required to attend Mass and Vespers in the Quire (the monks' part of the cathedral), participating either by playing the organ or by singing one of the parts as directed by the monastic Precentor. This duty sheds light on Wymond's involvement there a decade earlier. Stele was also required to sing one of the parts at the Mass of St Mary which was celebrated daily in the Galilee Chapel. His salary was to be £3. 6s. 8d. per annum, paid in two equal instalments, plus food, clothing, and there was the option of a house "within the Bailey". His contract also looked to the future, arranging that if his wife Isabella died and he did not re-marry then he would have the further accommodation option of "an honest room" within the monastery.

Stele was issued with a new contract on 2 January 1448.[9] The opportunity was taken to make a number of minor financial adjustments and to add "playnsange" to the musical syllabus, but the main reason was to provide for a situation which the first contract had not covered. It had appointed Stele 'for life', and it was now necessary to stipulate what would happen should old age or infirmity render it impossible for him to carry out his duties.[10] In that eventuality his allocation of bread and ale and his kitchen allowance would be halved, the ale being of inferior quality. As the salary formerly due to Stele was paid to the Prior from 1478 onwards it could be that he retired then. But as the payments are for the full amount, and no successor is named until 1487, he may have accepted the offer of accommodation within the monastery.

How soon the room which abutted the south end of the Nine Altars' Chapel began to be used as the choristers' schoolroom is not clear. According to *Rites* (p. 62) this room

---

[8] There was a local family of Steles - a John received payment from the Almoner in 1398-9, and tradesmen John and William were fined in 1424 by the Prior's Marshall (*Rolls*, ii, 367). The contract, in Priory Register III, ff. 137ᵛ-8ʳ, includes the earliest known use of the musical terms, 'pricknote' and 'faburden'.

[9] Priory Reg. IV, f. 60; *cf.*, J. Raine (ed.), *Historiae Dunelmensis Scriptores Tres* (Sur. Soc., ix; 1839), cccxv. See Locellus XXVIII, nos 15-16*, for the monastery's part of the actual indenture and for unissued duplicates for both parties.

[10] The timing of the second contract may have been prompted by the retirement in 1446 of John Wessington, the first prior to retire in over 120 years.

was very finely bourded within Rownd about a mannes hight about the waules and a long deske (did reache) frome one end of the scoole to thother to laie there bookes vpon, and the floure Bourded in vnder foote for warmnes, and long formes sett fast in the ground for the Children to sitt on. And the place where the mr did sitt & teach was all close borded both behinde and of either syde for warmnes.

The passage, which relates to the end of the monastic period, then states that these early choristers were six in number. It shows that the links with the almonry school had remained strong, for the boys "had there meat and there drinke of ye house coste amonge the children of thalmarie". It is highly probable, too, that they joined with them in the festivities involving the Boy Bishop, activities which have been referred to earlier. They may have also shared in the vigil kept when a monk died (*Rites*, 52):

Then were the chyldren of thaumerey sitting on there knees in stalls of eyther syd the corpes, appoynted to Read Dav: spalter [*sic*] all nyght ouer incessanly till the said our of eight a clock in the mornynge.

The children of the almonry were also responsible every Lent for burnishing the great brass candlestick, known as the Paschal, in preparation for Easter. This candlestick is reputed to have reached to the level of the triforium (*Rites*, 10, 17). More enjoyable, no doubt, were the occasions when the needs of the agricultural community caused school temporarily to be abandoned:

on bread and ale bought for the boys of the almonry for scattering, raising, and gathering hay, 8*d*. (*e.g., Rolls*, i, 236)

1487-1539: The later Cantors

Stele was succeeded in 1487 by Alexander Bell who had previously held brief appointments with two Oxford College choirs. He was followed by Thomas Foderley (in 1496), John Tildesley (1501) and Robert Langforth (1506). In 1512 the monastery entered into a contract with Robert Perrot of Magdalen College, Oxford, but an increase in salary persuaded him to remain there. During the search for a replacement William Robson deputized. In 1513 Thomas Ashwell was persuaded to leave Lincoln Cathedral. After Ashwell either died or moved on in *c*.1527 Robson became Cantor in his own right. How Robson, who was married, came to be so readily available has not been determined – he may have been one of the small group of adult singers or a former chorister of some ability. He was succeeded in 1535 by John Brymley, the last of the monastic Cantors. Brymley too may have been a former chorister.[11]

Compared with what Stele had done more was expected from his successors. They were required to give the instruction in two morning and two afternoon sessions, and to attend the *Salve Regina*.[12] Ashwell and Brymley were further enjoined to be present at the Mass of the Name of Jesus celebrated on Fridays at the Jesus Altar. This was the Nave Altar. It was located to the west of the stone screen which in monastic times connected the two western pillars supporting the central tower. Most significantly the Cantors after Stele were required yearly to compose

a new Mass of four or five parts, or something else equivalent to it ... in honour of God, the Blessed Virgin Mary, and Saint Cuthbert.

However, of some fifty Masses which must have been composed not even a fragment has survived at Durham.[13]

Rites sheds confirmatory light on the musical scene. It states (p. 62) that the Cantor played the organ in the Quire at the monks' High Mass and Evensong on principal Feast Days. At the same time as mentioning that the Cantor accompanied the daily Mass in the Galilee Chapel it records (p. 43) that "certaine decons & quiristers" assisted in its singing. There are also details (p. 34) about the Jesus Mass. During the service, which was sung by the Master of the Choristers and certain deacons, the choristers were in an organ loft which was situated between two pillars on the north side of the Nave. The loft had a stall on which the boys could lay their books. After the service was over the choristers "sat on their knees" before the altar and sang another anthem by themselves.

---

[11] For copies of their contracts, see Priory Reg. V, ff. 3^v-4^r (Bell), 142 (Perrot; named as Porret), 153 (Ashwell's 2nd) and 261^v (Brymley); *Script. Tres*, ccclxxxvi (Foderley) and cccxcviii (Tildesley); and F. Ll. Harrison, *Music in Medieval Britain* (1958), 429 (Ashwell's 1st). No trace has been found of any contract with either Langforth or Robson. There are payments to Robson's wife and son in the Bursar's account for 1533-4. The Brymleys were a local family, *cf.*, *Rolls*, i, 96.

[12] As the *Salve* was one of the antiphons sung at Compline, this may well be a way of referring to Compline.

[13] But see British Library, Add. MS 30520 B, f. 3^{r-v}, for Ashwell's, "Missa Sancte Cuthberte".

1539: Dissolution

In the late 1520s, some years before Henry VIII's dispute with the Pope, Thomas Wolsey[14] had been empowered by the Pope to merge or close some of the smaller monasteries and nunneries. The seeds had therefore been sown for the Acts of 1536 and 1539. These dissolved first the lesser and then the greater monasteries. For the monastic way of life the effect was as devastating then as the closedown today not just of a few plants but of the whole of an industry. However, some fourteen monasteries, including Durham, were destined not to become ruined reminders of their former glory, and for many of their monks there was the prospect of a secure future. These were the monasteries which were also cathedrals, the spiritual centres of dioceses. Thus, when the priory of Durham surrendered to the royal commissioners on 31 December 1539, its monks were aware that its role would be adapted to become like that of Norwich, which had surrendered in 1538 before the passing of the second Act, and like those of York, Lincoln and Salisbury, none of which had had monastic associations.

---

[14] Included among Wolsey's titles was Bishop of Durham. During his six-year episcopate (1523-9) he never visited the See, even being installed by proxy.

3. The New Foundation

1541: Re-constitution

On 12 May 1541, just over sixteen months after the monastery had surrendered, Durham was re-constituted a cathedral only. It must not be supposed that during that interval the cathedral was left like a ship without a crew. The maintenance of worship and the management of income were entrusted to about forty of the monks under Hugh Whitehead, the last Prior. At the re-constitution Whitehead became the first Dean, and twelve well-qualified monks became the first prebendaries [major canons], and others the twelve minor canons, the epistoler and the gospeller.

An accounting fragment relating to the later months of the interim period includes a payment to six unnamed lay clerks. Another describes John Brymley as the Master of the Choristers.[1] Neither, however, has any reference to any choristers. James Mickleton, an eminent local antiquarian active in the 1690s,[2] states that at the time of the re-constitution in May 1541 there were ten lay clerks and ten boys. Those boys he names as:

Christopher Mayer
Thomas Whitehead
William Sym
John Hunter
Edward Raw
Richard Stott
William Chapman
John Watson
Robert Biddick
Oswin Chapman

These are the earliest names of boys known to have been at the school. Whether any of them had begun their association in monastic times can only be conjecture, for the approximate date of birth of only one of them has come to light. He was William Sym, who later served as a lay clerk from 1558-9 to his death in 1572. Called to give evidence to the investigating commission following the Rising of the North in 1569, he stated that he was aged 40. This means that he would have been aged ten when the monastery

---

[1] Misc. Chs 2697 and 7283.
[2] Durham University Library, Mickleton and Spearman MS 32, ff. 28 and 56.

surrendered in 1539, and possibly too young to have been a chorister by then.[3] In his evidence he asserted that

> He haith not had to do with the teaching of any the queristers thes 4 yeres now last past.[4]

That there should be ten choristers was laid down in the cathedral's Statutes.[5] This was an increase on the number there had been in monastic times. That number was set at eight in the contracts with the Cantors, though according to the author of *Rites* there were only six.

As a result of Bishop Tunstall offering the Langley grammar school on 31 May 1541[6] to the new Dean & Chapter to meet the educational requirements of the Statutes it, and not the monastery's almonry school, became the new body's grammar school. At it there were eighteen free places. These were the original King's Scholars. Unlike today, they did not have to show academic prowess, nor in theory did it matter whom they might know. The criterion for their selection was that they should be "poor and bereft of the help of friends". Fifteen years was the normal age limit for admission to such a scholarship.

> Nevertheless we suffer the Choristers of the said Church to be admitted as scholars even if they have passed their fifteenth year; and we will that these, if they be suitable and shall have done good service in the Choir by their great proficiency in music, shall be preferred to the rest ...[7]

For the period 1541-1637 nearly a third of the 180 or so choristers went on to be King's Scholars, but between 1660 and 1900 only a few did.

As for those Choristers and their Master,

> We appoint and ordain that ... there shall be ten Choristers, boys of tender age and with voices tuneable and fit for singing, to serve, minister and sing in the Choir. For their instruction in gentle behaviour as in skill of singing, we will that, beside the ten [lay]

---

[3] See p. 22 for information about choristers' ages.

[4] J. Raine (ed.), *Depositions and Ecclesiastical Proceedings* (Sur. Soc., xxi; 1847), 150.

[5] As issued by Queen Mary on 20 March 1555. That these were replacements is evident from a deed (4.5.Reg.6) empowering Cuthbert Tunstall, the Bishop of Durham, and others, to correct, modify and improve those fomulated by Henry VIII. The new Statutes may have been necessary once the diocese, dissolved in 1551, had been restored.

[6] 3.3.Pont.10.

[7] *Statutes*, 145; and p. 143 for the two extracts below.

clerks before enumerated, one shall be elected, a man of honest report, of upright life, skilled in singing and in playing the organs who shall zealously give his time to teaching the boys, and chanting the divine offices. And that he may give his labour the more diligently to the discipline and instruction of the boys, we permit him to be absent from the Choir upon ordinary weekdays. ...

It should be noted that, as in monastic times, the boys were required to serve and assist in the celebration of services as well as sing. Even more was expected of their master. His own lifestyle was to be beyond reproach, and he was to be skilled as a singer and as an organist. His permitted absence on weekdays is significant, for it makes it clear that to start with the boys sang only on Sundays and Holy Days. This is not surprising in view of the small part the boys had played in monastic times, and, of course, it would be some years before there was a reasonable supply of music having a treble part.

Brymley himself did some composing for the new liturgy. Only part of the tenor part of his *Te Deum* and *Benedictus* survives, but complete is his stately and sonorous setting of the "Kerrie" (*Kyrie*; see p. 18), or, to be more accurate, Responses to the Commandments.[8]

The extent to which the Master of the Choristers was to be responsible for the "gentle behaviour" of the boys is then enlarged upon:

Let him take heed also to the welfare of the boys, whose education and liberal instruction in letters and at table and in their common manner of living we commit to his honour and industry. ... But if he be found negligent or slothful either in teaching or as regards the health of the boys, and not prudent and circumspect in educating them aright ... let him after threefold admonition be deposed from his office.

The which Master of the Choristers shall be compelled by an oath to perform his office faithfully in his own person.

In showing such cynicism about the frailty of man the formulators of the Statutes had the experience of what had happened in the non-monastic cathedrals on which to base their injunctions. Nor were they unjustified, for it will be shown that Richard Huchinson[9] had his troubles in 1627 and 1628, and that Alexander Shaw was ejected in 1681.

---

[8] Durham Cathedral, Music MSS C13; and E4-E11 and E11a. The texts of the *Te Deum* and *Benedictus* antedate those of the 1549 Prayer Book.

[9] This version of his name is found in the two latest Treasurer's Books, those for 1633-4 and 1635-6. Prior to that, as boy and man, 'Hucheson' was his usual rendering. 'Hutchinson' occurs only in the first quarter of 1635-6.

The treble part of John Brymley's Response to the 10th Commandment
(MS E4, p. 112; copied *c.*1630). The clef marks the position of middle C.

Equally, it was anticipated that inside the cathedral the behaviour of the
choir would be an area of concern. Accordingly, it was the duty of the
Precentor

> to control with decorum them that make music in the Church, to stir
> up the careless to sing, to reprove with moderation and to keep quiet
> those that make disturbance and run about the Choir in disorder, to
> examine the boys who are to be admitted to the Choir and are
> intended to sing ... . (*Statutes*, 135)

The writings of Dean Granville towards the end of the seventeenth century
(see p. 32) show that this was no exaggeration of the extent of possible
undisciplined behaviour.

In this respect it is interesting to note the custom of the choir processing
in orderly fashion both into and out of services is said to date back only to
the 1850s, when John Bacchus Dykes was precentor. Prior to that, the
arrival of individuals was haphazard to say the least. That some would be
late was construed as inevitable by the Statutes. They stipulated (p. 135) that
at Matins and Evensong those who had not arrived by the end of the first
psalm would be fined a farthing, as would those who had failed to appear by
the end of the *Kyrie Eleison* at Communion. The same penalty was also to
apply to those who for no good reason left before the end of a service.

18

Finally, it was hoped that the choristers, the free scholars at the grammar school, the eight poor men and the cooks would all wear outer garments of the same colour. As for the robes worn by the choir,

the rest of the Clerks and the boys in white surplices only. We will that no-one shall be compelled to wear black copes reaching to the heels. (*Statutes*, 159)

The latter practice must have been introduced by the reformers, for the accounts for 1545 include payments to John Brown "for makyng copys for the choristers & tunykylles" (*Rolls*, iii, 726-7).

1541-76: Life under John Brymley

Brymley survived many changes. Appointed in 1535, he had witnessed the end of the monastic period and the establishment of the new regime, and had seen English replace Latin as the language of the liturgy. Under Edward VI (1547-53) the reformers had gone further, and two new Prayer Books had been introduced. Then, under Mary (1553-8) the Pope had again been recognized as the Head of the Church in England. Finally, under Elizabeth I (1558-1603) the reformers had again gained the upper hand. Her 1559 Act of Supremacy had resulted in many clergy being deprived of their livings. Among them were Durham's Bishop Tunstall, Dean Robertson, and seven of the prebendaries.

William Whittingham, who was Dean from 1563 to 1579, was very much one of the reformers. A writer of hymns and co-translator of the Geneva Bible, the pattern of worship he introduced at Durham lasted for over 60 years. In a letter written in December 1563, he described the services in these terms:

First, in the morning at six of the clock, the grammar schoole and song schole, with all the servants of the house, resort to prayers into the church; which exercise continueth about half-an-hour. At nyne of the clock we have our ordinary service; and likewise at thre afternone. The Wednesdays and Fridays are appointed to a general fast, with prayers and preaching of God's word. The Sundaies and holydays before none we have sermons and at after none the catechisme is expounded.[10]

The choir, however, was not irrelevant, for, unlike many reformers, Whittingham did value the contribution that music could make, and

---

[10]   M. A. E. Green, "Life of Mr. William Whittingham" in *Miscellany VI* (Camden Society, civ; 1871), 23, n. 1, and pp. 22-3 for the next quotation.

was very carefull to provide the best songs and anthems that could be got out of the Queens chapell, to furnish the quire with all, himselfe being skillfull in musick.

A picture of what life may have been like for a chorister in Brymley's time is afforded by *Dobsons Drie Bobbes*, a book published in 1607.[11] It recounts the escapades of its 'hero', George Dobson, as a chorister, at the grammar school and at Cambridge. Even the name is genuine, for a George Dobson was a chorister from 1559-60 to November 1568, when he became a King's Scholar at the grammar school. Moreover, that the real Dobson was a colourful character is borne out by the Treasurer's Book for 1568-9. Although "Removed" against his name in the chorister section may not necessarily have sinister implications, that he is described as "a fugityve" after only half a term as a King's Scholar speaks for itself.

Dobsons Drie Bobbes so abounds in accurate local detail that Dobson himself must have been at least the source from which the writer obtained his information. Thomas Pentland, portrayed as Dobson's uncle, was indeed a minor canon, John Brymley the master of the choristers, and 'Barty' Mitford a local tradesman with a shop on Elvet Bridge. Various details in the book agree with the statements in *Rites* (pp. 97, 164) that the song school was then in the Sacrist's checker. This was an outbuilding situated in the angle between the north transept and the north aisle of the Quire. It had windows facing north and east, and the only access to it was through the now walled-up doorway in the north Quire aisle. Sound, too, is the choice of names for the two younger choristers who in one incident acted as Dobson's pages. Both Rakebaines [whom he calls James instead of Thomas] and [Matthew] Taylfar were several years junior to Dobson. Moreover, these two were not selected at random - they were indeed close friends and probably cousins. The friendship is confirmed by the bequest of a horse to Taylfar in the will of Rakebaines's father, the relationship pointed to by a mixture of details in the book and established facts. The book (p. 45) has Rakebaines, who it says came from a village some miles away from Durham, lodging with his mother's sister. It portrays his cousin – who is not named – as a chorister, and his uncle as a lawyer in the city. The Registers of the Dean & Chapter point to that chorister cousin being Matthew Taylfar, for they record that a John Telfer acted as its attorney on a number of occasions in the 1550s and 1560s.

---

[11] The edition by A. E. Horsman (1955) retains the 17th century spelling. In 1998 the School Play was *Pudding and Pie*, a dramatization by Stephen Drew, the Headmaster, of a number of Dobson's escapades.

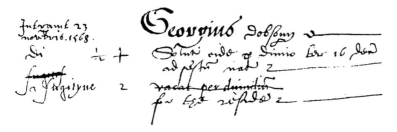

Treasurer's Book, 1568-9, part of f. 13^v

So much for the background; now for the incidents set in the Durham area. They may be fictional, but as Dobson did have to flee, they may contain more than an element of truth. Typical of schoolboy pranks are stealing Rakebaines's pudding, locking Rakebaines in a candle cupboard, persuading the rest of the boys to play truant while he himself went to school, causing his uncle's horse to be impounded and watering his uncle's ale. Contravening the law are buying some clothes at his uncle's expense, the theft of a goose and his pretence to be the son of the Chancellor of the diocese of Durham, a deception which obtained free meals at an inn in Witton Gilbert for him and his two page-companions. Spiteful, even evil, are the ways in which Dobson sought revenge – after his friend Rakebaines had been beaten for firing an arrow with malicious intent at Brymley's assistant at the song school Dobson arranged for that assistant to be caught by the Dean & Chapter in a compromising situation. Again, after his uncle had struck him for locking Rakebaines in the candle cupboard he had both his uncle and his aunt tied up overnight in their orchard.

Following the Rising of the North in 1569, Brymley and the other adult members of the choir were among those called upon to explain their part in a number of services held in the cathedral. Oliver Ashe, the Vicar of St Giles, testified that during Mass, at the time of the Elevation, "he loked up to Mr Bromley, then in the loft over the quier door, and smyled at hym".[12] Brymley, for his part, said that he had been present at two Masses. He claimed that he had not sung at these but had played the organ, and he admitted that he had been one of the singers at the 'Salve', Matins and Evensong. He also stated that he had "instructyd the choristers in such things as they dyd in the Quere, perteninge to service at that tyme, but not since nor byfore". Whether or not his heart had thrilled at the re-introduction of the old rite, his part, and that of the lay clerks, must have been adjudged those

---

[12]   Raine, *Depositions*, 137 and 148-9.

of subordinates obeying instructions, for no action was taken against them. Four of the minor canons, however, were deprived of their positions. Brymley died on 13 October 1576, at the age of 74. He was buried in the Galilee Chapel in front of the altar where in monastic times he had participated in the daily Lady Mass.[13] There this inscription marks his grave:

> IOHN BRIMLEIS BODY HERE DOTH LY
> WHO PRAYSED GOD WITH HAND AND VOICE
> BY MVSICKES HEAVENLIE HARMONIE
> DVLL MYNDES HE MAID IN GOD REIOICE
> HIS SOVL INTO THE HEAVENES IS LYFT
> TO PRAYSE HIM STILL THAT GAVE THE GYFT.

1576-1613: A Durham succession begins

With one enforced exception[14] all of Brymley's successors right up to 1681 had previously been Durham choristers. The first of these was William Browne, who became organist on the very day he ceased being a chorister. This is not as remarkable as might at first appear, for he had been a chorister for ten years, and was therefore at least 18, possibly 20 years old. This suggested age is supported by the fact that, for the period 1552-1637, only a handful of some 80 choristers whose dates of birth have been established joined the choir before their tenth birthday.

Mickleton described Browne as "An excellent Master of Musicke, a severe man" (*Rites*, 162). The former part at least of this description seems accurate, for several of Browne's choristers made some mark on the musical scene. Edward Smyth, Francis Dodshon, and Richard Huchinson were numbered among his successors at Durham, Cuthbert Byers became Organist at York Minster (1597-1604) and George Sheffield[15] spent many years as a Gentleman of the Chapel Royal (1610-41). George Rutter, William Whyte, Edward Smyth and Richard Huchinson were active as composers, and anthems by them were included in the Durham part-books and organ books copied during the 1620s and 1630s. Whyte, however, was not the Westminster Abbey lay clerk (1583-1603)[16] who composed fantasias

---

[13] His burial there is confirmed in the will of his nephew, Thomas Harrison, who died in 1582.

[14] Henry Palmer, who took over as Master of the Choristers in 1628 (see pp. 24-5).

[15] This version has been adopted as his last three attempts were all different.

[16] J. B. J. Saunders, 'English Cathedral Choirs and Choirmen' (Cambridge, Ph.D., 1996), p. 266.

for viols as well as anthems. He followed a different career, for Mickleton, writing about Miles Whyte, states,

> he was the father of William White, the celebrated doctor who lived in Elvet.[17]

Miles Whyte himself had been a chorister in the 1550s. As well as being a local miller, at the time of his death in 1611 he had been a lay clerk for over 50 years.

It also seems likely that Richard Nicholson, who was Informator and organist at Magdalen College, Oxford, from 1594 to his death in 1639, and whose origins have not hitherto been determined, was the Nicholson who was a chorister at Durham under Browne from 1576 to 1580.[18]

Browne served as Master of the Choristers from 1576 to 1588, and again from 1599 to certainly 1607, when he was persuaded to leave Durham for York.[19] Where he was between 1588 and 1599 has not been established. For that period lay clerk Robert Maysterman (1588-9) and minor canon William Smythe the Elder (1589-99), both former choristers, are named in the Treasurer's Books as Masters of the Choristers. It could be that Maysterman was only a stop-gap until an appointment was made, though, with Smith also a member of the foundation, it is also possible that Maysterman was not equal to the opportunity offered him. Whatever the truth about Maysterman, if he had not been replaced in c.June 1589 then he would have had to have been in September that year. In the short space of nine days during that month not only he and his wife died of "the plage", but also four of their six children. One of the two survivors was baby Ralph, who was only three months old. Touchingly, he was cared for at Chapter expense.[20]

William Smythe the Elder was energetic in his care of the organs. In his time a new set of "singing-bookes gylded" was acquired for the choir.[21] It was thought for many years that this Smythe was the composer of the responses, anthems, and other holograph works found under the name of William Smith in the old music manuscripts, but a comparison with

---

[17] So Mickleton MS 32, f. 56.

[18] This suggestion is the outcome of a query by Simon Anderson (chorister, 1976-81). For established details of that Nicholson's career, see H. Watkins Shaw, *The Succession of Organists* (1990), 380.

[19] J. Raine (ed.), *The Fabric Rolls of York Minster* (Sur. Soc. xxxv; 1859), 119.

[20] Post-Dissolution Loose Papers, 22/129, for 3 November 1590.

[21] His petition for payment for his work on the organ which was above the Quire doors is printed in *Rolls* (iii, 733); the payment for the music books in the Treasurer's Book for 1596-7.

signatures in the Treasurer's Books leaves no doubt that they are by a later Smith.[22]

Edward Smyth, who succeeded Browne in *c.*1608, was not related to William Smythe the Elder. He had been a chorister during Browne's second spell. It would appear from the Durham music manuscripts that he was quite active as a composer, but serious doubts have now been expressed about three of the attributions. In his unsigned will he left his best clavichord to his nephew William, about whom more will be said presently.

After Smyth's untimely death in February 1612 there was a short period of uncertainty. During it Francis Dodshon, another former chorister, appears to have acted on a temporary basis, extended from quarter to quarter.[23] Then, round about September 1613 Richard Huchinson, yet another of Browne's choristers, took over as Master of the Choristers. As for Dodshon, he remained on the Durham scene as a lay clerk until at least September 1617, at which point he became organist of Southwell Minster.

1613-46: Innovations and strife

How true is the saying, "The evil that men do lives after them; The good is oft interrèd with their bones"![24] Though Richard Huchinson was said to have been a first-rate organist, the Act Book records only his misdemeanours. He spent part of early 1627 in jail, but that did not have a salutary effect. On 1 April 1628 he was threatened with expulsion unless his behaviour improved. Mentioned specifically were his haunting of alehouses, and a brawl in one of them during which he seized a candlestick and brought it down upon the head of lay clerk Toby Brookinge, "wounding him verie dangerously". Matters still did not improve, and a month later, although a debt of £10 was written off, he was partially deprived of his office. It was decided

> that Richard Hutchinson orgainist shall henceforth totally relinquish the command, government, and teaching of the Quiristers. ... And further that the tuition of the said Quiristers shalbe wholie comitted unto Henry Palmer ... with full powre and authoritie of a maister or a governor over them, as well as for their voice and diligence in singing as for their manners & civilities in behavor, for which

---

[22] J. Buttrey, "William Smith of Durham", *Music & Letters*, xliii (1962), 248-54.

[23] Payments inside the back cover of the Treasurer's Book for 1612-13 confirm the assertion (*Rites*, 162) that Dodshon served for "about a year and a half". See Misc. Ch. 5916 for when Huchinson started.

[24] William Shakespeare, *Julius Caesar*, Act III, Scene 2.

purpose the Quiristers shall be bound to attend him onelie at their due houres.

Palmer, whose origins are not known, was one of the lay clerks. He continued as Master of the Choristers certainly up to December 1633, when he was paid the song school coal allowance, and probably until his death in September 1640. Huchinson's ability as an organist, however, was still valued, and he was instructed

> to be ready three tymes in everie weeke viz. on Tuesdaies, Thursdaies, & Saturdaies in the afternoone from twelve of the Clock unto the beginning of Evening prayer, and to teach the Quiristers to play upon the virginalls or orgaines and to be ready ... upon everie Sundaie or other convenient times ... to heare them play, for their skill & fitness in singing of any Anthem or Church Service.

The two passages are important for the information they provide about the choristers. In adjudging Huchinson an unsuitable example, they confirm that the provisions of the Statutes were being fulfilled, that the organist was indeed responsible for the entire education of the choristers. It is significant, too, just how much time was to be set aside to give the choristers organ and virginal lessons. The mention of instruction on the virginal is apparently the earliest evidence of any choristers anywhere being taught to play that instrument.

Hutchinson's partial deprivation did not bring him to his senses, and in July 1628 it was decided to he should be suspended from all his remaining duties in the cathedral until midsummer 1629. This ban was lifted after only four months.

The 1620s and 1630s were a period of great liturgical activity, for one of the prebendaries was John Cosin (Bishop of Durham, 1660-72). He was one of those who were dissatisfied with the existing pattern of worship, deeming it to lack both dignity and beauty. He re-introduced statues and vestments and reverencing the altar; and at Candlemas set up over 300 candles in the cathedral. Simply to label him a 'high-churchman' is to over-simplify, for he was even more anti-Rome than anti-Geneva. He was greatly interested in the role that music could play in worship, and it too became more elaborate. Eager to respond to the stimulus injected by Cosin, three members of the choir turned to composing. They were Henry Palmer and John Geeres (both lay clerks), and William Smith (a minor canon, formerly a chorister and briefly a lay clerk). This William Smith was Edward Smyth's nephew, the one who had been left his best clavichord. His setting of the Responses is still widely sung and highly regarded; and he also composed Responses to the Ten Commandments, Gospel Sentences, and Creeds, festal psalms, and anthems. Many of the anthems were settings of Collects proper to Feast Days or Sundays.

But while Smith may have responded with enthusiasm, it is clear from a statement Huchinson made to Parliament in 1628 that he was far from happy with the changes which had been made. He was not alone in disliking them. Nicholas Hobson, a veritable doyen of lay clerks, who by 1576 had become one of Brymley's choristers, was understandably set in his ways. In May 1642, when reputedly aged 92,[25] he set down his statement in writing. The seven months he had waited on Parliament's pleasure, and the long journey home, took their toll, for less than three weeks later he was dead.

As early as April 1627 a youth was paid to assist Huchinson by turning over the pages of the organ book. The organ itself was a splendid instrument installed in 1621. Its reputed cost of £700 was met not out of Dean & Chapter income but by Dean Hunt. Supplementing it were two cornetts and two sackbuts. These doubled at least some of the vocal parts. The noise made by the variety of musical instruments, together with the fact that the people could no longer join in the Psalms or the Creeds – nor could the celebrant himself say some of the Collects because they too had been turned into anthems – proved too much for Peter Smart, the senior prebendary. At the Calvinist end of the spectrum, his views on worship were diametrically opposed to those held by Cosin. For a sermon preached on 27 July 1628 Smart chose as his text, "I have hated them that hold of superstitious vanities".[26] His inveighings against Cosin and the practices he had introduced are recorded in the sermon, in his notebooks, and in various pamphlets he had printed.[27] They may have eased his conscience, but they quickly led to him being deprived of his positions, degraded from Holy Orders and imprisoned for about thirteen years. Eventually, in 1641, he was vindicated and restored.

In June 1633 Charles I visited the cathedral during his progress to Scotland. He attended various services, but was critical of the appearance of some of the outbuildings. Among these was the song school on the north side of the cathedral. As a result it was pulled down, and a temporary school was set up in the south transept.

---

[25] For Huchinson's and Hobson's statements see V. Staley, *Hierugia Anglicana*, ii (1903), 225-8. With regard to Hobson's age, even if he were 20 when he ceased as a chorister in March 1580, he would only have been 82 in 1642.

[26] Psalm 31, v. 7 – it is v. 6 in modern psalters.

[27] His notebooks (Rawlinson MSS A441, C584, D821 and D1364) are in the Bodleian Library, Oxford. His printed works include *A Sermon preached in the Cathedral Church of Durham* (1628), *A Short Treatise of Altars* (1629), and *Canterburies Crueltie* (1643).

It is probable that the custom of the choir singing anthems on top of the tower dates from the 1630s, with Cosin as its instigator. Tradition has long asserted that originally the choir went up to commemorate the battle of Neville's Cross, fought on 17 October 1346. Why the choir sings three anthems, one facing north, one facing east, and one facing south, but not one facing west, is apparently because the monks who had gone up the tower were afraid to look in the direction of the battle. Such an explanation not only flies in the face of natural curiosity, it ignores the fact that the monks, with the banner of St Cuthbert, were in attendance at the battle. Tradition also asserted that after the formal recognition of Charles II as King on 29 May 1660, the date was changed to 29 May, and the Restoration and the victory were celebrated at the same time.

Although Durham's extensive records confirm that the choir did sing on the tower on 29 May from certainly 1672 until 1968,[28] they afford no evidence of any commemoration of the battle. The Durham custom, however, does go back before the Restoration, for the Treasurer's Books disclose three payments to the choir for singing there in the 1630s – on 5 November 1633, 27 March 1634, and 5 November 1634. Those dates, too, had strong royal associations. 5 November was, of course, when the plot to blow up King James I and his Parliament was discovered, and 27 March, the 'King's Day', was the anniversary of the accession of Charles I. That the Church should mark such days stemmed from the fact that the monarch was the Head of the Church of England. The cathedral's archives show the anniversaries of the accessions of Elizabeth I and James I being observed with bell-ringing and bonfires, whilst additional to one set of part-books used by the choir in the 1630s are anthems for 5 November and for The King's Day.[29]

When Cosin in 1635 added the Mastership of Peterhouse, Cambridge, to his preferments, he took with him Thomas Wilson, who had just left the ranks of the Durham trebles, to be his College Organist. Wilson was very active there as a composer, but only his setting of "By the waters of Babylon" – an anthem not in the Peterhouse choir books – is among early additions to the Durham books. In 1638 John Foster, when still a chorister, composed a Service which was immediately included in the repertoire.[30]

---

[28] Between 1660 and 1672 the records lack thoroughness. From 1969 onwards, apart from 1985 to 1992 inclusive and 1998, when Ascension Day was chosen, the choir has sung on a Saturday near 29 May. For a review of the tradition see the *53rd Annual Report of the Friends of Durham Cathedral, 1985-6*, 24-6.

[29] *Cf.*, Music MS C2. Durham still has 29 music books from this period.

[30] He is so described, and the Service so dated, in Music MS A5, p. 224.

Suddenly, this high summer of Durham's musical activity was over. In September 1640, following the defeat of the King's army, the Scots over-ran Durham. Their occupation of the city lasted until August 1641. Towards the end of their stay they began to wreck the organ, with the result that under the cover of night its pipes were removed to safety. It is said that the Dean fled; but he and at least six of the prebendaries met regularly in Durham in late 1642 and 1643. The Act Book records the appointment of two lay-clerks during that period,[31] but makes no reference to any choristers. Indeed, in the absence of any Treasurer's Book after 1636 or schedules relating to the triennial Episcopal Visitations after that of 1637, one can only assume that there was still a group of them.

1642 and 1643, however, were just a brief respite, for greater storm clouds were gathering. In 1643 Cosin was impeached by Parliament, and early in 1645 the use of the Book of Common Prayer was proscribed. As it is not known how quickly this measure took effect at Durham, it is not possible to tell whether Huchinson's last years – he died in 1646 – were spent in enforced idleness. Moreover, there is no way of determining whether his successor was appointed or even contemplated.

---

[31]   Mickleton, MS 32, f.56^v names them and also a further two.

4. Post-Restoration

1660-1710: A new beginning

The restoration of Charles II to the English throne marked the resumption of cathedral worship. In November 1660 it was agreed that ten oak trees should be felled and left to season over the winter, and that new choir stalls and seats should then be fashioned from them. The old stalls had perished during the Commonwealth period, though it is now thought unlikely that they were burnt by the Scots who were imprisoned in the cathedral in 1650 and 1651.

On All Saints' Day (1 November) John Barwick was installed as Dean. Mentioned as present at his installation were "2 Masters of the Quiristers",[1] a remark as frustrating as it is intriguing, for no names are recorded. It may not be explained away as the remark of one unfamiliar with the cathedral hierarchy, for it is in the hand of Elias Smyth, who had been a minor canon since 1628. Whoever the two may have been, it was John Foster, the former chorister, who was appointed Master of the Choristers and Organist at Christmas 1660.

In March 1661 eleven [*sic*] new and completely inexperienced choristers were selected. In June/July 1661 a small organ obtained by Bishop Cosin for £80 in London was tuned by lay clerks John Nicholls and James Smart. At the same time, negotiations were being conducted between Dean Barwick and George Dallam for "one fare double organ". A price of £550 was agreed upon on 5 October 1661, and the work was completed by Christmas 1662. It is said that Dean Sudbury, the new Dean, was annoyed that the little organ was used on Christmas Day in preference to the new one. His displeasure did not go unheeded, for on St Stephen's Day, the very next day, Foster played the Dallam organ for the first time.

The song school moved again, this time into accommodation under the Monks' Dormitory and to the south of the Spendement.[2] There it remained until the end of the nineteenth century. An inventory of movable objects in

---

[1]   The information in this and the next paragraph is taken from Hunter MS 125, p. 223, and *Rites*, 162-4.

[2]   There are two rooms there now. What was a third room (and the men's vestry) became in 1978 the north end of the Treasures of St Cuthbert Exhibition. In the 1890s the room nearest the Spendement was the actual Song School, the other two music rooms (see p. 60). A century earlier Chrishop had been allowed to live in presumably them (see p. 38).

the cathedral has been dated at *c.*1665.[3] It includes a section on the song school. In it were "Two Deskes and two Backseates" and "One Foulding Table". Mentioned too are the "Two Sackbutts and Two Cornetts" used in the earlier part of the century. They had not become museum pieces, indeed the two cornetts had been played by two anonymous boys at Dean Sudbury's installation. Again, in 1664, as soon as their treble voices had broken, Alexander Shaw and Matthew Ridley transferred to the sackbut and cornett respectively. The sackbuts continued in use until 1680, and the cornetts reduced to one in 1696, Ridley playing the other – or holding the sinecure – until his death in March 1698.

The Inventory also lists what music books were in the choir stalls and organ loft, and what could well be described as the text-books used by Foster in his training of the boys. Included are *Introduction to Musick* by Morley and [*The Triumphs of*] *Oriana*. As most of the books had been published late in the sixteenth century or early in the seventeenth, it is likely that Foster himself had been 'taught' from them in the 1630s.

In 1662 Bishop Cosin conducted his first Episcopal Visitation of the cathedral. One of his Articles of Enquiry asks,

> Doth the Master of the Quiristers (or Organist) diligently teach and instruct the tenne younge Choristers every day in their Schoole; doth he attend divyne servyce dayly in the Quire habit, as the other singing clerkes doe, and looke that all the Quiristers doe the same, every one keeping their gownes and surplices cleane and behaving themselves orderly, reverently, and decently during the whole tyme of divyne servyce in the Quire?[4]

Those for 1665 add,

> Do the same Choristers provide & place Song-books ready, as they are appointed by the Precentor in every Quire-mans stall before service time, while the bells are tolling, so that they have no occasion to go from their seats, and pass to & fro in the Quire during the whole time of Divine Service?

Though the questions were answered in the affirmative, the reply of Prebendary Isaac Basire in 1668 hinted that all was not well. Having noted that "judicious strangers" had said "that the service of god is better performed here than in sundry Cathedrals", he added, "yet I wish some effectuall course were taken for <u>the better</u> breeding of ~~better~~ choristers". Basire

---

[3] B. Crosby, "An 17th-century Durham Inventory", *Musical Times* (1978), 167-70.

[4] Hunter MS 11, gatherings 78, 94 and 112 respectively for the Articles of 1662 and 1665, and for Basire's answers in 1668.

weighed his reply carefully, for he inserted the words which are underlined above to replace what he had crossed out. But, being alive in the seventeenth century, discipline and social background were his concern, not genetics.

It has already been shown that a number of choristers maintained contact with the cathedral after their voices had broken by becoming lay clerks, instrumentalists, organists and minor canons. Others took up similar appointments elsewhere. One position not mentioned so far was with the Bishop of Durham. In a letter dated 16 October 1669, William Flower, the Bishop's chaplain, instructed Miles Stapleton, the Bishop's secretary, to

> speake to Mr Nicholls and Mr Foster, Organist of Durham, to see if they can prepare a boy to play well upon the organ against My Lord comes down into the country.

The matter was not attended to immediately, for some months later Bishop Cosin complained,

> Nor doe you tell me whether Mr Nichols or Mr Foster hath provided me with a new organist boy since Francke ranne away.[5]

Nicholls is mentioned first because he had since 1667 been master of the Langley song school, a position which the Bishop supposed was in his donation.[6] That Frank was Francis Forcer, the only chorister of this period to have that Christian name, is confirmed by the Bishop's Household Book.[7] It names Forcer in the position from February 1666 to September 1667. With certain payments in the London section to a Mr [John] Hingeston (formerly of York) for giving Forcer music lessons it is clear that Frank did not run away to London but from the Bishop's residence there. He became one of the organists at Dulwich College and married in London in 1673. There he was active as a composer of instrumental music, and at his death was a partner in Sadlers Wells. One anthem by him found its way into the Durham repertoire in the 1690s.

Foster died in 1677. Although in his will he claimed to be other than wealthy, the inventory of his possessions mentions three houses in Gilesgate, an organ, 3 virginals, a dulcimer, 2 bass viols, 2 violins, and a 'cittraine'. In his place Alexander Shaw, the former chorister and sackbutter, who had disappeared from the Durham scene in 1672, was appointed Organist, but not Master of the Choristers as well. That position was given to the John Nicholls who has already attracted notice. Nicholls's action of providing a

---

5 G. Ornsby (ed.), *Bishop Cosin's Correspondence*, 2 vols (Sur. Soc. lii, lv; 1869-72), ii, xxxvi and 232.

6 For proof that Cosin was mistaken see above, p. 16.

7 Sharp MS 163. Forcer was a chorister, 1661-5.

deputy at the Langley song school affords proof that the two schools were quite distinct and that the title to the Langley school had not yet degenerated into a sinecure. Where Shaw was between 1672 and 1677 is uncertain. As he copied part of a Ripon music book now in the British Library (K.7.e.2), he may well have been the Shaw who was organist at Ripon in the first half of 1677.[8] His relationship with the Dean & Chapter of Durham ran even less smoothly than Richard Huchinson's, for on Christmas Eve 1681 he was "ejected for contumacy".[9] The Act Book, however, gives no indication of any trouble at that time. Shaw, who had married Foster's widow, was content to remain in Durham. The notice of his wife's burial in 1701 describes him as "organist", and that of his own in 1706 as "musician".

Durham's earliest Service Sheet, listing the settings of the canticles and the anthems sung each day, belongs to this period. Manuscript, it is for June 1680, and is stuck inside the front cover of one of the bass part-books (MS C17).[10] Though imperfect, it confirms that Matins and Evensong were sung each day by the full choir. On Wednesdays and Fridays there was no anthem at Matins. In the 1960s, when Matins was still being sung on Tuesdays and Thursdays, eight settings of the morning canticles and seven of the evening ones, but only two anthems, were still in the repertoire.

By 1681, as the writings of Dean Granville show,[11] the behaviour of the whole choir left much to be desired:

5ly. Boyes running up and downe the Quire rudely and unseasonably [*sic*], without any manifest necessity or reason, and sometimes quite contrary to command.

6ly. The Quiristers carrying Anthem Bookes and sometimes Common Prayer-bookes very impertinently and troublesomely to those that do not desire nor need them. ...

8ly. The Quiristers, and sometimes the Singing-men staring, gazing, and laughing, indecently lolling, and sometimes scandalously sleeping not only during the sermon but also the service.

9ly. A great part, if not the greatest part, of Singing-men and boyes many times not joining at all in the responses, and sometimes not at all in the very Creed and Lord's Prayer, or at other times gabling them over, and outrunning the Precentor and others of the Quire.

---

8 Ripon, Registrum A, p. 103 – now in the Brotheton Library, Leeds University.
9 "Ejectus ob contumaciam" has been added by Mickleton to his MS 32, f. 55[v]. The date in the MS is more precise than *Rites*, 162, which has "at Christmasse".
10 B. Crosby, "A Service Sheet from June 1680", *Musical Times* (1980), 399-401.
11 R. Granville, *Life of Dean Granville* (1902), 249.

Appointed as successor to Shaw was William Greggs, the Master of the Choristers at York. With him Durham introduced 'new blood', for unlike all initial appointments since the death of Brymley in 1576 he had not served his musical apprenticeship as a Durham chorister. Mickleton's assertion, that Greggs commenced his duties on Christmas Eve 1681, the very day that Shaw was expelled, raises the question how Greggs came to be so readily available. It is possible – though with the Treasurer's Books for 1680-1 and 1681-2 not extant, and the Act Book silent, it can be no more than a conjecture – that Greggs was already the Durham Master of the Choristers. According to Mickleton, when Nicholls, who had been appointed to that position in 1677, died in June 1681, he was succeeded by Robert Tanner. Although Nicholls signs for all four payments in 1679-80 Tanner's name does appear above that section, possibly as a guideline for a later book. Again, the lack of the next two books means that the length of his stay can not be determined.

It is not clear either, whether Shaw was removed from his position as quickly as Mickleton supposed, for organ book MS A1, p. 334 has, with the date in Greggs's hand, the double holograph inscription:

Mr Will: Greggs

Alixander Shaw

Jan the 5th 1681[*i.e.,*1682]

Greggs features a number of times in the Chapter Act Books. In 1686 he was given three months leave of absence to go to London to improve his skill in music; in 1690 he was granted £10 to enable him to buy the Langley song school; in 1697 he was remunerated for composing an anthem to celebrate a national victory; and in 1704 he was "admonished to be more careful in his teaching of the choristers". One of his earlier choristers, Thomas Allinson, clearly learnt his lessons well, for in May 1693 he resigned the lay clerkship he had progressed to at Durham to become organist at Lincoln. That position he held until his early death in 1705. At Lincoln he was succeeded by George Holmes, another former Durham chorister. In 1698 Holmes had been organist to the Bishop of Durham.[12]

Set now in the outside south wall of the Quire of the church of St Mary the Less, Durham, is part of Greggs's gravestone. It must be in error in giving his age as 48. He had been at York before coming to Durham, and whilst it is not inconceivable that he was only fifteen when he was appointed Master of the Choristers there in 1677, he can hardly have been "expert in

---

[12]   British Library, Add. MS 31446 at one time included the comment, "George Holmes his Book, 1698 at my Lord Bishop of Durham's".

music" and appointed a singing-man there in 1670 at the tender age of eight![13]

1711-1811: Two long 'reigns'

This period of one hundred years saw only two Masters of the Choristers – James Hesletine (1711-63) and Thomas Ebdon (1763-1811). Hesletine had been a chorister under John Blow at the Chapel Royal. In September 1707, some three months before his voice broke, he composed "Unto thee have I cried", a verse anthem.[14] He was already organist at St Katharine's Chapel near the Tower of London when at the age of 19 he was appointed to Durham. He had the reputation of being an able composer, and the words of seven anthems by him are given in *A Collection of Anthems ... Durham*, 1749.[15] Of those anthems only "Praise the Lord" is found in sufficient of the cathedral's music books as to permit reconstruction.[16] This regrettable situation prevails because, it is said, Hesletine himself destroyed as many of his compositions as he could lay his hands on, supposing that he had been slighted by the Dean & Chapter. The only suggestion in the Chapter Act Books of any friction was in 1727, when Prebendary Thomas Mangey reported that Hesletine had behaved offensively towards him, and the threat of suspension was imposed unless an apology was forthcoming. This incident, however, would appear to be too early.

Hesletine must have derived some income from teaching private pupils, for in June 1730 he was given "leave for Three Months from this day to Teach one day in the week in the Country". An example of the sort of musical instruction he used to give the choristers was in 1992 discovered rolled up in a small hole in the plaster on one of the walls in what used to be the song school off the western side of the cloisters. Written in Hesletine's hand on each side of a small piece of paper are exercises based on ascending and descending fourths.[17]

In March 1748 Hesletine was given permission to go to Finedon, Northants, for three months while the Durham organ was being rebuilt, and to take three boys with him. Finedon was the family seat of Sir John Dolben,

---

[13] York, Chapter Acts, 1634-1700, ff. 82^v and 114.

[14] A holograph copy of this survives as British Library, Add. MS 30860.

[15] Durham Cathedral Library, Printed Music A6.

[16] But a copy of "O let my mouth be filled", a solo anthem, copied for his nephews, has returned to the Library as Music MS M206; see also footnote 14 above.

[17] Now in the keeping of the Cathedral Archeologist (see also p. 52).

one of the prebendaries of Durham. There they were joined by one of the lay clerks and a minor canon. The instruction of the remaining boys was entrusted to lay clerk Cuthbert Brass. Then, in September 1748, with Hesletine hardly back from Finedon, it was

> Order'd that the Room over Sir John Dolben's Gate [? now the archway outside the present school] be Fitted for a Song School to teach the Singing Boys in.

As Hesletine was already living in Dolben's house[18] it seems likely that the room was so fitted out, though it is doubtful whether it served such a purpose after Sir John's death in 1756.

One of Hesletine's choristers went on to fame and fortune. He was Stephen Paxton, whose two older brothers – Robert and William – became Durham lay clerks. Like William he had music lessons in London, but in London he stayed. There he made his name as a 'cellist and as a composer of music for that instrument. A successful glee composer, on four occasions he won one of the Gold Medals awarded annually by the Noblemen and Gentlemen's Catch Club. He was associated with the Sardinian Embassy Chapel, and in 1779 rated his three Masses as his best compositions. When he died in 1787 he was said to be worth over £10,000. His brother William won Catch Club Gold Medals on two occasions (both posthumous!), and was involved in the concert scene in Durham, Newcastle, and York. Their orphaned nephew, George, left the Durham choir early to join Stephen in London. From 1767 to 1775 he was organist at the Sardinian Embassy Chapel. Later, he became a member of the Drury Lane Theatre band.[19]

Information about some of the services held in Durham Cathedral comes from the diaries of the Revd G. W. Harris, the Rector of Egglescliffe and a Canon of Salisbury Cathedral.[20] For Evensong on Thursday, 9 November 1752, Harris has "I know that my Red[eeme]r. Hebden", and for Sunday, 12 December 1756, "Hercules. I will look, &c." Hebden is none other than Thomas Ebdon, to whom belongs the other 'long reign'. As Handel's *Messiah* had by then been copied into the Durham music books, it looks as if Ebdon (then aged 14) sang the solo. The solo sung by Edward Harculas has not been identified.

---

[18] Northumberland Record Office, NRO 452/C3/5, includes a letter from Sir John Dolben dated 18 April 1744.
[19] The careers of the four Paxtons are examined in B. Crosby, "Stephen and other Paxtons" (*Music & Letters*, February 2000), 41-64.
[20] Harris was Rector of Egglescliffe, 1740-77. See D. Burrows and R. Dunhill, *Music and theatre in Handel's world: the family papers of James Harris, 1732-1780* (2000), 284 and 320.

Cuthbert Villans

Anno Domini 1747

T Ebdon Sepr 1755

Graffiti (both reduced)

A number of the choristers, particularly those of the 1740s and 1750s, carved their names on the woodwork which at the chancel steps separates the Quire from the Quire aisles. Most magnificent and carved carefully in a cursive style is Cuthbert Willson's contribution (see opposite). As it is on the Quire side of the woodwork one wonders how he escaped detection! Persistent though not as artistic was Thomas Ebdon – he carved his three times, little realizing what his future role would be!

Born in Durham in 1738, Ebdon served the cathedral for over 63 years. He was admitted a chorister in April 1748. The organ was then being rebuilt and Hesletine was away at Finedon. At Michaelmas (29 September) 1756 he progressed to being a lay clerk, and from Midsummer to Michaelmas 1763 he acted as organist after Hesletine's death.

The decision in October 1763 to appoint Ebdon Master of the Choristers was not without its controversy. The Act Book records that he was very much the Dean's choice, elected "*contra consilium* [= against the advice] of everyone of the Prebendarys present in Chapter". In November 1764 it was ordered that this statement be erased, but the instruction was so worded that it has resulted in the statement's perpetuation!

One wonders whether the prebendaries were protesting at the Dean exercising his prerogative, rather than that they had serious doubts about Ebdon's musical ability or the extent of his commitment. That said, it is nevertheless true that his sacred compositions display little flair; and in his early years they were well outnumbered by at least nineteen harpsichord concertos and sonatas. Showing a certain facility of composition but no originality, these today would be classified as 'easy-listening'. As for his commitment, the prebendaries would have been aware that he was already involved in the local concert scene.[21]

It was in Ebdon's time that it was felt necessary to introduce additional instructors. It is far from clear whether in doing so the Dean & Chapter were enlightened ahead of other ecclesiastical authorities, or whether they were driven to it by Ebdon's inability, incapacity, or lack of interest.

From Michaelmas 1775 Thomas Robinson, a lay clerk who had been a chorister until June 1775, acted as "Director and assistant-Instructor of the Choristers in the Choir", his additional salary being £15 per annum. Then,

---

[21] Ebdon's various activities and compositions are examined in Simon D. I. Fleming, "A century of music production in Durham city, 1711-1811: A critical and documentary study" (Durham Ph.D. thesis, submitted in September 2008). During his assessment of the concertos and sonatas (draft version, p. 374) he expresses the opinion that Ebdon 'put more effort into writing secular music'.

from 1782 to 1785, while he was still a chorister, John Banks was paid for his "Assistance in Teaching the choristers". In November 1785 it was "Agreed that Ralph Banks as Teacher of the Choristers Have the same Salary (£4) as was Given to his Brother". He too was still a chorister, and must have been quite successful, for in November 1788 it was agreed that he be continued as Assistant Master in the song school at £20 per annum "after his Time ceases with Mr Ebdon". Ralph's destiny, however, lay elsewhere, for in 1792 he was appointed Organist of Rochester Cathedral (see p. 41, n. 7).

In December 1797 it was "Ordered that Mr Chrishop be allowed to Purchase himself a Bedstead, chairs, and a Table for the Song-School"! Chrishop, presumably the George Chrishop who was organist at Staindrop $c.1789$,[22] was duly refunded his £13 expenses, and the items were regarded as fixtures, though they were later granted to him. From 1796-7 to 1802-3 he was paid £10. 0s. 2d. per annum "for Teaching the Boys", and during the same period the payments for music copying were made out to him and not to Ebdon. Consequently, the comment, "George Chrishop Organist of the Cathedral Church of Durham", in one of the tenor part-books (MS C15, p. 213) may well indicate the practical truth of the situation. In addition to this, in April 1799 lay clerk [Charles] Stanley was appointed "to Teach the Choristers Reading & Writing in the Song-School", his salary being £16 per annum. This duty he undertook seriously, and later the same year submitted a bill "for Books, Pens, &c for the Choristers". In November 1801 it was agreed that another bill should be paid, but he was advised that in future it should not be for more than £5. From May 1802 until at least June 1803 the teaching of reading and writing devolved upon lay clerk [James] Radcliffe. Then, in March 1804, [Ralph] Harle, a former chorister, was appointed "Schoolmaster for the Choristers".

Since then, the Organist, though still retaining the official title of 'Master of the Choristers', has had little to do with the general education of the boys, which aspect from this point onwards increasingly dominates their lives.

---

[22]   So the list of subscribers to Thomas Ebdon, *Sacred Music*, vol. 1 ($c.1789$).

5. The growth of academic awareness

The early nineteenth century

In February 1801 George Sewell, one of the choristers, was "dismissed for several crimes alledged by his Schoolmaster, & also contumacy in refusing to obey a Summons to attend Chapter". The failure to exercise sufficient control over the boys had a fatal consequence a few years later. At an unspecified date between 29 September 1806 and 29 September 1807 the records disclose that workmen were paid 12s. 8d. for "Attending the Corpse of the Chorister killed by a Fall from the Cathedral".[1] Although this entry merely accounts for expenditure, and the tragedy does not feature elsewhere in the cathedral archives, the *Newcastle Courant* for Saturday, 27 June 1807, includes this informative paragraph:

> On Thursday evening [*i.e.*, 25 June 1807], a boy named Thomas Avrick [*i.e.*, Averick], aged 11 years, one of the singing boys of the cathedral at Durham, when in search of bird nests in one of the western spires of the cathedral, fell, and was killed on the spot.[2]

However, although the report answers a number of questions, it also raises one, for there is no other evidence of any Averick ever being a Durham chorister.[3] Particularly telling in this respect is the fact that he was not one of the ten boys who signed for their quarterly stipends on 20 June 1807, just five days before Averick died. The probable explanation is that, although there were only ten paid choristers, there were other boys, including Averick, who attended practices and received schooling and possibly even sang at services.[4] Over thirty years were to elapse before such a situation received official sanction. It was agreed in June 1841 that three boys should be chosen as supernumeraries with possible promotion to the choir. Among the successful early supernumeraries were William J. Peele and David Scott. A travel book names them as choristers in 1843 even though they did not progress to the paid ranks until 1844 and 1845 respectively.[5]

---

[1] Audit Book A.VIII, p. 418 (for 1806-7).
[2] *Op. cit.*, p. 4, col. 3.
[3] The suitably aged Thomas Averick, baptized at Whickham on 26 June 1796, could have boarded in Durham. The reporter may have been misinformed about there being spires on the western towers – though 'spire' can also mean 'top'.
[4] Two much earlier supernumeraries were Anthony Brignell and George Maddison. They received small payments as such in 1694-5 and 1695-6.
[5] T.S.M [Thomas S. Muir], *A Ramble from Edinburgh to Durham* (1843), 129.

That Averick was looking for birds' nests may have been something of a cover story, for in July 1807 some of the boys stood accused of stealing lead. It is not known what punishment was meted out; but it is significant that the Dean & Chapter felt itself partly responsible. It resolved to review the regulations for apprenticing choristers whose voices had broken, and also to make provision for their better general education. The meeting of 20 November 1807 considered the choristers' financial remuneration. It was decided to impose a qualifying age. Boys who left the choir before the age of thirteen would not be entitled to an apprentice fee.[6] For those who continued after their thirteenth birthday their annual 'salary' would be increased by £6 to £16, and, subject to satisfactory progress, they would receive the greatly increased apprentice fee of £20 when they left. The Treasurer's account show that two boys received the salary increase that term and that three others joined them during the course of the financial year. To avoid any abuse, it was decided in March 1816 that the apprentice fee would no longer be paid to the boy or his parents but to the boy's 'master', and then only on production of an indenture. This requirement was modified in January 1819 when the Chapter reserved to itself the right to allocate the fee in the way it thought best.

The provision for a better general education followed on 21 November 1807. It was something of an anti-climax, for Chapter merely stipulated that "[Thomas] Clamp the Head Quorister be allowed further the additional sum of Four Pounds per annum for superintending the other Boys". This was hardly a new situation, for since the 1780s (see pp. 37-8) senior choristers and lay clerks had been similarly employed. Clamp acted as 'superintendent' until February 1811 when he was dismissed for felling trees in the plantation at Shincliffe. Other 'superintending' head choristers were John Tomlinson (1812-14), Thomas Brown (1814-17) and Matthew Brown (1817-18).

The behaviour of the boys continued to give cause for concern, and in October 1820 it was felt that an example had to be made. It was

Ordered that James Hill a Chorister of this Church being convicted on the complaint of the Precentor, the testimony of the senior chorister and his own confession of irreverent behaviour at Church after repeated admonition & punishment be considered incorrigible and as such be, and he is hereby, expelled from his situation in the Choir.

Copies of this order were sent to the boy's father and to the Precentor. It was also read out to the other boys, and a copy was put up in the song school.

---

[6] Apprentice fees can be traced back to March 1688 when William Sherwood received £3. From 1702 £2 seems to have been the usual amount.

The Precentor, it will be remembered, was responsible to Chapter for selecting the boys and also for their behaviour in the cathedral, duties he was reminded of in May 1823. Hill was not the only chorister to meet such a fate, for in January 1823 John Brown also suffered expulsion.

In December 1820, and possibly as a result of the Hill incident, lay clerk Thomas Brown, the most recent superintendent of the boys, started receiving £20 per annum "for teaching the Choristers in the Song School, reading & writing". Whatever limitations he may have had, he did at least bring some continuity to the scene, for he held the position until 1864.

It was shortly after Brown had been appointed that the Dean & Chapter was approached by Miss Maria Hackett (1783-1874). The daughter of one of the prebendaries of St Paul's Cathedral, London, she devoted her long life to endeavouring to improve the lot of all cathedral choristers. She was not so much concerned with the musical side – deplorable though that was in many places[7] – as with the general neglect and abuse of the boys. The sole concern of many cathedral authorities was that the boys should be in their places during services. No thought was being given to how they spent the rest of the day; certainly they were not receiving any general education, neither was provision made for them once they left the choir.

The Dean & Chapter's reply to her questions was factual, with many phrases echoing the Marian Statutes:

> The number of the Choristers is ten, and they are chosen by the Precentor, subject to the approbation of the Dean and Chapter. They are obliged to attend divine service in the Abbey twice every day, at 10 of the forenoon and 4 in the afternoon. They are allowed two suits of clothes annually, and receive a salary of between £8 and £9 in money, with other perquisites, which may make the above amount to £10. The organist teaches them music from eight to ten o'clock every morning in the song school, situated in the Cloisters, and occasionally at other times, but is not allowed to derive any emolument from their talents; they have besides, a master, who teaches them reading, writing, and arithmetic, in the same school, at such hours as do not interfere with the organist. They are generally admitted very young; that is, as soon as it can be ascertained that they have an accurate ear and a good voice, and are of course discharged

---

[7] Ralph Banks (see p. 38) recorded in one of the Rochester organ-books, "When I came from Durham to the Cathedral in 1790, only one lay clerk attended during each week. The daily service was chanted. Two Services (Aldrich in G and Rogers in D) and seven Anthems had been in rotation on Sundays for twelve years" – so Watkins Shaw, *The Succession of Organists*, 238.

as soon as the voice breaks. There is no provision for them afterwards, though such of them as have behaved well are not neglected by the Chapter.[8]

No exaggerated claims are made, and the details of the services and practices are interesting. Though it was only as recently as November 1820 that the annual provision had been increased to two suits each at a total cost of £50, clothing (a requirement of the Statutes) had been provided for over 50 years. In November 1764 Mr Hogg, the Clerk of the Works, had been instructed to supply each boy with a coat, waistcoat, and breeches, the total cost being limited to £15. Two years later it was agreed that the boys should be so equipped every year. The cost was increased to £20 in 1796 and to £25 in 1815. Apparently, in the early part of the nineteenth century the suits were dark brown, the waistcoats red.[9] The boys' health had also been attended to from certainly the 1730s; and in 1786 the apothecary had been instructed to examine them every quarter. Ever since Charles Stanley's bill in 1799 there had been regular payments for "Books for the Choristers", even though before 1850 it was rarely over £6. In 1825, for instance, it was agreed to provide them with "Spelling Books", the cost being limited to £1.

One is surprised that the reply made no reference to the two-tier salary scale, only an average figure being given. The last sentence of the reply does not contradict itself – its first clause refers to the educational scene, its second to the apprentice fee. Regrettably, it spoke true, for even though the boys had a teacher, his restricted experience meant that the education imparted was of the most elementary nature.

Between 1830 and 1850 the Dean & Chapter showed itself to be well in the van of educational development. It was party to the foundation of the University of Durham in 1832, and to setting up the Diocesan Training School (later Bede College) in 1841. Next to receive attention was Durham School, which had been on Palace Green (in what is now the University Music Department) since 1661. It was moved to its present site in 1843.

That something had to be done about the choristers was highlighted by a complaint made in June 1846 by William Henshaw who had been Organist and Master of the Choristers since 1814. He was perturbed by the behaviour of the boys, who were neither punctual in their attendance at song school, nor obedient either there or in the cathedral. The situation was investigated;

---

8   M. Hackett, *A Brief Account of Cathedral and Collegiate Schools* (1827), 22.

9   J. T. Fowler, "Durham Cathedral Choristers' School", *The Cathedral Quarterly and the Church Music Review*, iii, no. 12 (1916), 10. This information had been obtained from Canon Greenwell and a Mr [Thomas] Jones. The latter had been a chorister [1834-42], and remembered being measured for the clothing in the cloisters. The oil painting to which Fowler refers has not been found.

and the report which the Dean & Chapter considered in July 1847 dealt with the expediency of providing the choristers with a better education. They were told that whereas the current annual expenditure on the choristers was £270, it would not be possible to board them in a separate house and maintain the efficiency of the choir for less than £460. However, the boys' parents said that they preferred the existing system, even though in order to compensate for the educational deficiencies a number of them were sending their sons to evening school at their own expense. In the circumstances it was agreed that the existing situation would not be subjected to any immediate alteration.

Choristers, *c*.1840 (detail from
R. W. Billings, *Durham Cathedral* (1843), Plate XLV)

Nevertheless, the opportunity to make improvements continued to be looked for. It presented itself in July 1849 when the role of the next Precentor was considered. It was decided that he would be resident and not responsible for a parish as well, and that either he or some other approved clergyman would supervise the boys' religious and moral education and examine them twice a year as to their general learning. The association of such a person with the school would also make some instruction in the Classics possible. This was to take place at times which did not conflict with the boys' other commitments. The Dean & Chapter agreed to advance £1. 1s. 0d. a quarter in each instance, provided that the instruction was likely to be profitable, that it was given by the Precentor or some other approved clergyman, and that the parents contributed a like sum. In July 1858 the Organist was permitted to give instrumental tuition at the same rate.

At the same time it was resolved to increase the annual salary of boys under twelve years of age to £17, and of those over twelve to £27, subject to satisfactory progress. Some of this increase on expenditure was to be offset by the parents becoming responsible for every expense (*e.g.*, clothing and medicine) except the provision and washing of surplices.

That the emphasis was now very much on promoting the academic side is demonstrated by a change made to the apprentice fee. This was still to be £20 for boys who went into trades or became craftsmen. However, if a boy went on to the grammar school he was to receive £15 a year for two years, irrespective of whether or not he qualified for a King's Scholarship. Equally, if he went to the Diocesan Training School, or attached himself to the Organist or any other professor of music £30 was to be spread over three years. One chorister who was articled to Henshaw before the apprentice fee was increased was John Young. In 1850 he became Organist and Master of the Choristers at Lincoln, duties he continued to fulfil until he retired in 1895. Other choristers who became organists included Richard Ingham, James Stimpson, and Samuel Reay.[10]

The new Precentor, appointed in November 1849, was the Revd John Bacchus Dykes. Some of his hymn-tunes are still popular today.[11] Dykes immediately started receiving payments for "Classical Tuition". In his half-yearly report given in February 1853 he stated that in most respects the education given at the Choristers' School was highly satisfactory, though there were areas (not specified) where additional instruction was required. What those aspects were may be gathered from the appointment the very

---

[10] Ingham at Carlisle Cathedral (1833-41), Stimpson at St Andrew's Church, Newcastle (1836-41), at Carlisle Cathedral (1841) and at Birmingham Town Hall (1842-86) and Reay at Newark Parish Church (1864-1905).

[11] Including *Dominus regit me* (The King of Love my shepherd is), *Melita* (Eternal Father, strong to save) and *Nicaea* (Holy, holy, holy, Lord God Almighty). He also composed a setting of the Burial Responses and several anthems.

next month of W. H. Engledew[12] to assist Thomas Brown by taking Geography and History. The notice of Engledew's resignation in September 1856 described him as "Assistant Teacher of the Choristers".

September 1856 also saw a further 'official' increase in the number of boys.[13] Although the number listed in the main part of the Treasurer's Books remained at ten, it was now decided that there should also be eight probationers, up to four of whom were to receive two shillings per week. To qualify for this sum a boy had to be over eight years old, to have been a probationer for over a year, and to have made "fair progress ... & be, in other respects, a promising well-conducted boy". Probationers were not guaranteed places in the choir, and if after fair trial backed up by quarterly examinations held by the Precentor they did not appear likely to become efficient choristers they were to be removed from the school.

However, although boys could be removed for not making satisfactory progress as well as for misbehaviour, it must be remembered that those who continued until their voices broke were given financial assistance to enable them to continue their education or enter into an apprenticeship. Moreover, Chapter showed a positive interest in the boys' health. In May 1842 a doctor was requested "to attend to Brown one of the most useful Singing boys who is now suffering from a sore throat".[14] Again, in September 1864, the parents of Thomas Kaye were given £20 to enable him "to go to the sea for a change of air in order to restore his health".

At the end of December 1862 Henshaw retired, having completed exactly 49 years as Organist. In his place the Dean & Chapter appointed Philip Armes, the Organist of Chichester.

Probably shortly after Henshaw retired[15] a paper was drawn up describing his role with the choristers. He had attended on them in the song school from 8.30 to 9.50 a.m. There he had rehearsed the music for the day in one room with the older boys. One of the older boys, however, had taken the younger boys in another room. They spent the time there learning the

---

12   Engledew was followed by Richard Forster (Sept. 1856–June 1858), R. L. Kirby (June 1858–1859), T. Smith (1859–Dec. 1859), William Davidson (Dec. 1859–Sept. 1861) and Thomas Deighton (Sept. 1861–Dec. 1864). Engledew, possibly a King's Scholar at the Grammar School in 1829, had been an assistant master at the Blue Coat School and "Writing Master at the Grammar School"; Forster had also held the latter position, Davidson and Deighton the former.

13   Chapter approved the action on 4 October 1856.

14   There were three chorister Browns at the time – Thomas, John and William. Of these William, who had only joined in September 1841, can be eliminated.

15   DCD/P/AE (formerly St Helen's 208). The watermark on the paper includes the date '1862'.

rudiments of music, the Confession, the Lord's Prayer, 'the Belief', the responses and the psalms for the day.

On Saturday afternoons there had been a regular additional practice from 2.30 until about 3.45 p.m. when the music for the Sunday was rehearsed. On other afternoons the younger boys were occasionally required for an hour's practice.

The paper then set out the changes to be considered by the Dean and Chapter. It was suggested that the boys would be fresher at their school lessons if choir practices were held in the evening, and from 5.00 to 6.00 p.m. was put forward as a possible time. It was also proposed that in the summer the practices should be in the song school, when part of the time would be spent on all the boys becoming familiar with the words of the items mentioned above, but that in the winter they should take place in the organist's house, possibly from 6.00/6.30 to about 8.00 p.m. There the Confession would be rehearsed, but most of the time would be spent practising musical exercises and learning new anthems.

The conclusion stressed that Henshaw had been careful to ensure that the boys did not learn pieces off by heart or sing them by ear; and that he had been at great pains to ensure that all the boys were thoroughly grounded and practised in notes and in the scale.

It seems unlikely that the proposed changes were ever introduced, for in 1897 the first activity of the day was still a choir practice (see p. 56).

In February 1864 Thomas Brown also retired, bringing to a close an association of 56 years with the cathedral. His final salary as a teacher was £30 per annum. The opportunity to appoint a qualified teacher was not taken, for Brown's successor, on £42. 12s. 0d., was David Lambert, another former chorister who had become a lay clerk. In August 1865 he was informed that his services as a teacher would not be required after Christmas. He continued as a lay clerk until his death, which occurred during Evensong on 30 October 1873.

1865-76: The Lawsons: the first qualified teachers

Lambert's successor in December 1865 was Richard Lawson, a master at the Blue Coat School, Durham. He was a qualified teacher, and had recently completed a course at the Durham Diocesan Training School.[16] This was reflected in his salary, which at £61 per annum was more than twice that earned by Thomas Brown just two years earlier. Richard soon died, and in November 1866 his brother Joseph was appointed master of the choristers

---

[16]   From the records of the College of the Venerable Bede.

"for the purpose of their general education". His salary was £70 per annum plus six shillings per quarter for each boy taking Latin.

That Joseph Lawson did not combine his duties with any other occupation emerges from the *Returns relating to Cathedral Establishments* produced at the request of the Ecclesiastical Commissioners in 1867. The Dean's return (*op. cit.*, 89-90) discloses that there were fourteen choristers in all. The details of what they were paid show that this comprised ten full choristers, some of whom were above twelve years old, and four paid probationers. The unpaid probationers are not mentioned. At this stage the boys were neither boarded nor lodged at the expense of the Chapter (though this did not preclude some of them doing so at parental expense). Their school is described as a "special school", distinction being made between it and the "cathedral school" (*i.e.*, Durham School).[17] In reply to the question about assistance for the choristers who had left, the Dean stated that over the last seven years the yearly average had been £45.

In 1872 C. M. Carlton compiled a *History of the Charities of Durham & its Immediate Vicinity*. In the course of reviewing eligibility for scholarships at the grammar school he states:

> In the case of Choristers, though exceeding 15 [years of age], "they are allowed to be admitted as Scholars, and, if duly qualified, and had made good proficiency in music, and faithfully served in the Choir, it was ordained that they should be chosen in preference to all others." At the present time, and for many years previously, no Chorister has ever attempted to obtain this privilege, although special provision is made for their admission, "if duly qualified." The reason is apparent, the education imparted entirely precludes boys belonging to the Song School from ever attempting to obtain such a valuable appointment. (*op. cit.*, 79-81, 84; see above, p. 16)

His remarks show that musical contribution was no longer a consideration, that academic grounding was the real criterion for selection; and he explains why the choristers' education left so much to be desired. It was because until a few years previously it had been so narrow – "The organist taught music; and one of the Lay Clerks taught the elements of English".

The pages above show that that was not entirely correct. The curriculum had been broadened by the inclusion of History, Geography, Scripture and some Latin; and other significant improvements would have been made had the parents supported Chapter's proposals. Be that as it may, Carlton's

---

[17] The close relationship between the cathedral and Durham School was broken in the 1990s.

description of the contemporary scene reads well as a prospectus. Emphasis is laid on the fact that

> A properly qualified master is now appointed who devotes all his time to the work. The Dean and Chapter have fitted up the School with apparatus, and supplied each boy with a complete set of the very best School books and other requisites. .... In addition to the usual elements [presumably Reading, Writing and Arithmetic] they are taught Drawing, Mensuration, Euclid, Algebra, book-keeping, and Latin.

Carlton names the schoolmaster as Joseph Lawson, and states that he had ten choristers, four supernumeraries, and four probationers in his charge. This, too, is not wholly correct, for in c.June 1871 yet another Lawson, Thomas, had taken over. His salary was £82, and when he resigned at the end of June 1876 it was in order to become ordained like his brother.

That the boys' education was now being undertaken seriously – rather than that their handwriting was proving to be illegible – may have been one of the considerations which led to the cathedral's Service Sheets being produced differently. Chapter decided in November 1872 that in future these would be printed instead of being copied out by the boys.

In October 1875 two of the choristers, Henry Revely and William C. Sarsfield, succeeded in 'emulating' some of the adult members of the choir – they were reported to Chapter for being drunk! As a result, they were suspended for the rest of the year, and informed that the apprentice fee customarily paid to choristers when they left would in their cases be halved. Each of them was also set a task by the Precentor. Revely completed his and was restored – and when the time came he was articled to the organist at the full apprentice fee – but Sarsfield did not as he was withdrawn by his father.

6. The search for an identity

1876-1901: Improvements in many directions

Henry P. Meaden became Schoolmaster in July 1876. He was already known to Chapter, for as Master of the St Oswald's School he had been given permission in August 1872 to borrow books from the Dean & Chapter Library. The greatly increased salary of £130 indicates that he was well qualified. He had received the later stages of his education at Chester Training College (1853-5), and on the completion of his course there had been taken immediately on to its staff. He was one of the first group of certificated Science teachers in this country, and had been elected a Fellow of the Chemistry Society in 1863.[1]

Evidence of the standard of education provided has survived in the form of a few examination papers. These include the Latin paper set at Christmas 1876. It is hand-written, but specially printed are the Euclid paper for 1879 and the Latin papers for December 1880 and Christmas 1890. The 1876 and 1890 Latin papers were for the Senior Division and were of two hours' duration.[2] The exams were marked by an external examiner who reported his findings to Chapter. The arrangement into two divisions continued until 1948. Apart from Latin (not necessarily studied by everyone, and in 1849 entrusted to the Precentor or some other cleric), Meaden taught both groups himself.

Belonging to this period, and found behind the plaster when a wall in the cloisters song school was examined in 1992, is a fragment of a handwriting exercise. The exercise teaches more than handwriting, for the imperfect sheet is headed, 'PH[YSICS]'. In spaces left for that purpose the pupil has made two copies of printed master versions which run:

The unit of weight is [the] kilogramme. It is nearly equal to [two] and a fifth pounds Avoirdupois.

The unit of capacity is the litre, [a] measure about equivalent to 1¾ [pints]. A litre of water weighs one kil[ogramme].

---

[1] Information communicated by Mrs Margaret Wilson. A Meaden herself, her sons Mark (1976-81) and Alexander (1982-8) were day-boys at the school.

[2] See pp. 50-1. The examination papers are held by the Cathedral Library.

CATHEDRAL CHORISTERS' SCHOOL.

EXAMINATION—CHRISTMAS, 1879.

EUCLID.

1.—Define 'point,' 'straight line,' 'plane superficies,' 'plane rectilineal angle,' 'right angle,' 'isosceles triangle,' 'right-angled triangle,' 'acute-angled triangle,' 'circle,' 'square,' 'rhombus,' 'parallel straight lines,' 'trapezium.'

2.—What is an axiom? Give any three you can remember.

3.—Write out the Postulates.

4.—

A B and C D are straight lines, and E F falls upon them.
How do you know whether A B and C D are parallel or not?

5.—From a given point, draw a straight line equal to a given straight line.

6.—If the two sides of an isosceles triangle be produced; the angles thus formed at the other side of the base are equal to one another.

7.—If two angles of a triangle are equal to one another, the sides also which subtend or are opposite to the equal angles, are equal to one another.

8.—What do you mean by 'data,' 'hypothesis,' 'problem,' 'theorem,' 'proposition,' 'definition,' 'corollary,' 'Q.E.F.,' 'Q.E.D.,' 'postulate'?

CATHEDRAL CHORISTERS' SCHOOL.

EXAMINATION, DECEMBER, 1880.

LATIN GRAMMAR.

1.—How many declensions of nouns are there in Latin? How are they distinguished? Decline in full one noun of each declension.

2.—Decline jusjurandum, respublica, vis, magnus dux, vastum mare, parvula virgo.

3.—Turn into English

 (i.)—Naves hostium sunt celeres.

 (ii.)—Ira furor brevis est.

 (iii.)—Miles comitem hastâ occidit.

and into Latin

 (i.)—The troublesome boy has many stones.

 (ii.)—The king gives rewards to the soldiers.

 (iii.)—The lion has a strong body.

4.—Conjugate the verb "sum."

5.—How many degrees of Comparison are there?

 Compare "acer," "parvus," "senex," "bonus," "malus."

6.—Write out the future indicative, present subjunctive, imperfect subjunctive, future perfect, and the infinitive mood of "amo," "moneo," "rego," "audio."

7.—Decline "ille," "ipse," "ego," and the "reflexive" and "relative" pronouns.

8.—Translate into English

 Prudens magister puerum improbum, qui librum delevit, castigavit: sed puerum industrium laudavit. Huic tria mala, illi baculum dedit.

Athletic Sports, 1886

Event	Prize	Won by
Throwing Cricket Ball (Seniors)	1. Book	[C. F.] Bulmer
Long Jump (Juniors)	1. Honey Jar 2. Butter Knife	[G. V.] Stafford W. Bulmer
Long Jump (Seniors)	1. Stationery Cabinet 2. Wedgewood [sic] Jelly Dish	[?P.] Nicholls [C. F.] Bulmer
100 Yards Flat Race (Juniors)	1. Horn Cup 2. Cricket Ball	[B. C.] Goodhead W. Bulmer, not [F. L.] Thompson
100 Yards Flat Race (Seniors)	1. Cup 2. Two Pictures[3]	[?P.] Nicholls [C. F.] Bulmer
High Leap (Juniors)	1. Book 2. Two Salts	1. [F. L.] Thompson 2. [G. V.] Stafford 3. [B. C.] Goodhead
High Leap (Seniors)	1. Brass Flower Vases 2. Silver Albert	[?P.] Nicholls and [G.] Newby 3. [A.] Parkinson
Quarter Mile Race (Juniors)	1. Cup 2. Inkstand	[G. V.] Stafford W. Bulmer
Half Mile Race (Seniors)	1. Desk 2. Cruet 3. Fishing Rod	[A.] Parkinson [L. M.] Shadforth [B.] Race
Consolation Race	1. Book 2. Pocket Knife 3. 4.	[A. J.] Tuke [C. H.] Nutton [A. W.] Read [?W.] Nicholls

Among other items found behind the plaster are a fragment giving a few tenses of the passive voice of 'lego' and a page of a Geometry exercise done by 'H. Reed' (chorister, 1894-8). In those days exercises consisted of writing out theorems and their corollaries – and Reed was not accurate.[4]

Life was not all singing and academic lessons. Some time was given to physical activities, and the Potter's Bank field was allocated to the school in July 1883. By then there was already an annual Sports Day held on the University [Racecourse] Cricket Ground. The Programmes for June 1883

---

3   The two pictures won later by Thomas Dixon (1897-1902) were old prints of the cathedral. His daughter, Mrs M. Howe (d 1999) showed me them in 1998.
4   The last three items are held by the Cathedral Archeologist (see also p. 34).

and 1884 list the events, the prizes, and the competitors for each event. They show that all ten boys in each division entered every event for that group. Handwritten lists dated 1886, 1889, 1894, and 1895 give details of the events and their prizes, and name those who won the prizes.[5] As the list opposite shows, the prizes for first and second places were worth winning. The cup presented in 1883 to the winner of the Senior 100 Yards was a silver cup. This is known because George Bailes, its winner, later gave it back to the school. By far the school's oldest trophy, it is still awarded each year to the winner of the equivalent race.

In April 1892 the Precentor sought Chapter's permission to broaden the choristers' curriculum by including gym. He had already sounded out the instructor at the Y.M.C.E.A. gymnasium[6] at 85 Claypath, and was able to report that the cost would be £4 for 12 one-hour sessions. Chapter agreed, provided that the choristers were taught separately by a properly qualified instructor. Thus began John Levesley's long association with the school, an association which was to last until his retirement in 1948. He was then in his 80th year. Of him Headmaster Ganderton then said, 'he has never seemed to age, and until a year or two ago, he could still do amazing things in the Gymnasium'.[7]

Since about 1700 Chapter had helped the boys financially when they left the choir, no matter whether they continued their education or entered apprenticeships. In January 1883 it was decided that the interest from the £200 collected as a memorial to Archdeacon Bland should be used to provide prizes for the choristers. Its original purpose was to enable a leaving chorister to buy the books needed at his next school. By 1885 the recipient of the Bland Prize was receiving a book with the Bland arms embossed in gilt. In 1916 the results of the school examination and usefulness in the choir were the determining factors. The prize, though not in book form, is still received by leaving choristers on Speech Day.

In April 1883 the question of the boys having some leave of absence was raised by Archdeacon Hamilton. It was agreed two months later that there would be one afternoon each week when the boys would have no cathedral commitments. Previously they had sung Matins and Evensong every day. At

---

[5] The Sports Day programmes and lists were given to me by James Fenton (chorister, 1957-62; Newdigate Professor of Poetry, Oxford, 1994-9) when he was sorting through papers which had belonged to Canon Ganderton. They now form part of the Chorister School archive (references, DCD/P/AD and P/AE) deposited with Archives & Special Collections, Durham University Library.

[6] The 'Young Men's Church of England Association', later the Y.M.C.A.

[7] H. Y. Ganderton, *The Chorister School* (c.1968), 103.

first it was Wednesday afternoons which were free, unaccompanied Evensong being moved to Fridays. What is not clear is whether, as in the early 1900s, there was holiday from school as well.

In July 1884 Chapter considered the whole question of payments to the boys while they were still in the choir. Because junior probationers were not paid at all and there were different rates for senior probationers, junior choristers and senior choristers, and because promotion depended on when other boys' voices broke, the total amount being received by choristers varied considerably. Where some boys had over a five-year period received as much as £110, others had received only £35 to £40, and two boys, Lawes and Hodgson, who were then aged 13½, had "never received sixpence". It was, therefore, proposed that for the first 2½ years the yearly rate should be £12 a year, and after that, £20. This would mean that every boy who was in the choir for five years would receive £80.

Of major concern was the unsatisfactory state of the surroundings in which the choristers were receiving their education. Still serving as their school, as it had done since the 1660s, was the room off the western aisle of the cloisters. Then there were only ten boys, now there were twenty. Writing in 1915 about the school Canon Fowler recalled that the room was

> so narrow that, with the large bookshelves on both sides of it, the two rows of boys were almost singing into one another's faces, a bare four feet separating them, and with the door at one end and the window at the other, colds were a constant trouble.[8]

As has already been mentioned, Chapter had tried to do something about this in July 1847, but the proposal to set up a boarding house had been rejected by the parents (see pp. 43-4). That conditions needed improving was again brought to the fore in a letter from the Precentor to Chapter in September 1881. It prompted Archdeacon Watkins to offer the use of two rooms in his house. Although Chapter approved his offer it is not known whether it was taken up. Certainly, the situation continued to be turned over, for in November 1881 Chapter informed the Precentor that, although it appreciated that improvements were needed in lodging and other areas, it could not increase the current yearly expenditure of £600. The door to progress, however, was not closed, for it added that it would consider any schemes that he might have.

The matter surfaced again in July 1884 when the money received by the choristers was reviewed. That meeting was also informed that the distance

---

[8]   J. T. Fowler, "The Durham Cathedral Choristers' School", *Cathedral Quarterly*, iii, no.9 (1915), 8.

they lived from Durham had resulted in two promising boys being excluded from consideration for the choir. In August 1885 there appeared to be light at the end of the tunnel, for it was stated that the unexpected death of one of the minor canons who lived in the precincts now allowed steps to be taken to establish a boarding house. Once again, however, those steps were for some reason delayed.

But boarding did in the meantime become possible. In May 1887, having sacked his lay clerk father on account of drunkenness, Chapter determined that the son, Benjamin Charles Goodhead, should board at Chapter's expense – though where this was is not stated. In September 1890 it was agreed that new chorister Joseph Ellison should board with Meaden, who lived in South Street, and it was not long before others joined him.[9]

The situation relating to the choristers was one of the areas about which the Articles of Enquiry circulated by Bishop Westcott in 1893 requested information in connection with the Episcopal Visitation scheduled for November that year. He sought clarification about the provision made for the choristers' religious and general education, and wondered what proportion of them progressed to the grammar school. He wished to know what provision was made when they left; and what had become of those who were choristers in 1883. Finally, he enquired whether the buildings used were adequate, and whether there was any provision for boys who lived at a distance.

Chapter's reply of 20 July stated that the general education was entrusted to a qualified master, and the religious education to the precentor. Very few proceeded to Durham School, even though assistance with the fees was available. Chapter did help the other leaving choristers too, granting £20 on evidence of an apprenticeship or other employment.

The reply then listed what had become of the twenty choristers of 1883:

1 dead	1 clerk in the Dean & Chapter
1 organist	Land Agent's office
1 shipbroker's clerk	2 stationers' assistants
1 chemist's assistant	1 teacher of music
1 banker's clerk	1 draper's assistant
1 engineer	1 brass finisher
1 ironmonger's assistant	1 student at Durham University
1 solicitor's clerk	1 currier
1 post office clerk	1 music dealer
	1 in Canada

---

[9] Over the next dozen pages the decisions reported in the Act Books have been fleshed out by new information found in the papers referenced under P/AA.

55

Returning to the choristers' general education, Chapter added that it supervised what the Headmaster was doing, and would seek the Bishop's approval should any major changes be contemplated. It stated that provision was made for those from a distance, but conceded that the buildings were barely adequate, and undertook that it would turn its attention to the choristers and their school once the restoration of the Chapter House had been completed.

The Visitation itself must have prompted further questions, for in December 1893 Chapter re-iterated to the Bishop that there was a separate master who was responsible for "the entire grammatical and literary teaching of the boys in the Choir". It added that the organist's only contact was in the sphere of music; and it made it clear that boys going on to the grammar school received £30.

The restoration of the Chapter House was completed in June 1896, and in March 1897 Chapter appointed a sub-committee to report on the state of the school. On 1 May it was agreed to circulate that report. When it was considered on 5 June, the sub-committee was instructed to prepare a further report on boarding and education. The committee acted promptly, and its report drawn up on 17 June was presented to Chapter two days later.

It began by stating the existing timetable,

Music	8.30 – 9.45 a.m.	School	2.15 – 3.15 p.m.
Cathedral	10 – 11 a.m.	Church	4 – 5 p.m.
School	11 a.m. – 1 p.m.	Music	5 – 5.45 p.m.

and concluded,

Your Committee is of the opinion that the hours given to general Education are too short, and that those given to Music (Song School) are too long.

They suggest that as soon as may be the Song School should be in the same building with the Day School, and that time table might be as follows:

School	8.30 – 9.30 a.m.	School	2.15 – 3.45 p.m.
Music: Scales &c in the Sch: Room	9.30 – 9.45 a.m.	Cathedral	4 – 5 p.m.
Cathedral	10 – 11 a.m.	Music	5 – 6 p.m.
School	11 a.m. – 1 p.m.		

It noted that there was no school on Wednesday afternoons, and expressed the opinion that "there might be an hour in the Evening at any rate for boarders; or the boys would go in the Evening to the Science and Art Classes".

Analysis shows that with the proposed timetable the choristers would be spending three and a quarter hours on Music and Cathedral compared with four and a half in School, where in the past the figures had been four and three hours respectively.

The report also considered the subjects being taught, and suggested that a distinction might be made between those taught throughout the school, and those which might be called Technical and taught only to those boys who showed aptitude. In the former it placed (A) Religious Education (the Bible, Church Services, Catechism), and (B) Reading and Writing, Arithmetic, elementary study of the English Language, a start to French or German, English History and Geography, and Drawing; and in the latter, Music for all the Choir boys, Higher Music (Piano, Violin, &c), Classics for promising boys (possibly at the Grammar School), Higher Maths, Engineering and other technical subjects (Chemistry, Hydrostatics – to be taught in the Science School) and Higher Drawing.

Consideration was also given to staffing. It recommended that

1. the present Headmaster, who had given 23 years' service,[10] should be pensioned off at £86. 13s. 4d, which was two-thirds of his salary;

2. in future the Headmaster should have £100 per annum and a house rent free, and that he should accept some boarding pupils, say 4, rising to 5 or 6, for each of whom he would be entitled to £27. 10s. 0d. per annum;

3. the assistant master should be paid £80 per annum;

4. the advertisement for the next Voice Trial should draw attention to the fact that the most promising of the four successful candidates would qualify for free education, board and lodging, and that the other three would be charged only £15 per annum.

The sub-committee estimated that the proposals would cost Chapter about £200 more than was currently being expended; and suggested that those living in the town should have the option of being day boys or boarding at £15 per annum. It also felt that only those having the necessary ability should become Foundation Scholars at Durham School, but that for others going there the Dean & Chapter should pay £15 per annum and not just for two years as in the past.

---

[10] As Meaden had been appointed in 1876, he had served but 21 years.

Finally, the sub-committee recommended that there should be a new committee consisting of the Dean, Canon Kynaston, the Precentor, the Organist and the Revd J. L. Bennett (minor canon, 1893-1901), who had been appointed assistant organist in January 1897. This extended Bennett's involvement with the choristers, for in February 1895 he had been invited to help Dr Philip Armes, the Master of the Choristers and Organist, with the training of the choir for the next two years, and to deputize on the organ whenever Armes was absent.[11] Armes and Bennett worked conscientiously, and in November 1900 submitted a report to Chapter on the hours when the choristers received their musical instruction (including playing the organ) and from whom.

At its meeting on 19 June Chapter agreed that the advertisement for the Voice Trial on 8 July 1897 should offer the suggested incentives, and it instructed that it should be placed in *The Guardian*, *The Church Times*, *The Record*, the two Durham papers, *The Newcastle Daily Journal* and *The Musical News*.[12] It also agreed to the proposed new sub-committee.

The information included in the advertisements was also conveyed in a printed brochure issued under the Dean's name and dated July 1897. It added that the boarding places would be available at the house of the minor canon who was also assistant organist [*i.e.*, Bennett], and that the education provided would be such that those with the appropriate ability would be able to continue their education. The intention was that the Choir School would become "a place of technical education, in which Music shall be the special subject; Classics, Mathematics, Science, Art and Literature in various degrees, the subjects of their general teaching."

However, it is not clear whether the brochure was ever circulated, because on 3 July, after applications had closed, Chapter determined to postpone any appointments to the choir. Then, on 20 July, it decided to appoint probationers in the usual way, and to refer back the report presented on 19 June.

A year later, in July 1898, the sub-committee was asked to explore the possibility of providing a purpose-built song school on the site of the revestry.[13] A report was presented to Chapter on 5 November 1898, but consideration of it was referred to the meeting on 19 November. The report

---

[11] Choristers were boarding with Bennett, who in February 1898 was told he could spend up to £5 on games for them; and that this grant could recur.

[12] A cutting in DCD/P/AA confirms that the advertisement was placed.

[13] This had been off the south Quire aisle, opposite the organ (see p. 7)

and plans were then accepted, but the final decision was left to the meeting of the Great Chapter, as was the proposal made on 3 December that a passageway be constructed from the slype to the new song school.

The fact that the deliberations were on-going did not mean that the old song school continued to be used, for on 15 October 1898 Chapter informed the Bishop that the old song school had been closed and that a new one was in use, but that further improvements were being considered. This it stated in reply to the Articles submitted in connection with a Visitation to be held in the November. It also reported that one chorister had been entered for a scholarship to the grammar school, but had not reached the standard required. Nevertheless, he had gone to the school, where his fees and those of another former chorister were being paid by Chapter. To the Bishop's questions about the training of choristers, the possible strain of services, and holidays no response was made.

The hope of the meeting on 15 October was that as soon as possible practice would be held in the school. Precisely where the school was then is not clear, for after it left the cloisters its first temporary home was in what had been the servants' hall under the Deanery. After that, the spacious dining room of a prebendal house, then partly occupied as the Diocesan Mission House, became the setting for both the musical and academic instruction.[14] In January 1899 the ladies living on the floor above complained of the inconvenience caused by the singing practices. This resulted in the whole question of suitable accommodation for the school being considered yet again. In the meantime the basement of the Deanery was brought into use. The Deanery was fortunate to escape serious damage after the boys found some sticks of dynamite on Prebends' Bridge. It was thought that all the sticks had been confiscated, but one found its way into a pile of coke and from there into the boiler. The boiler door was blown off with such force that a door opposite was smashed and the solid walls cracked. Fortunately, no-one was injured.[15]

It was also in January 1899 that Chapter heard that the architect had costed the proposed new song school and passageway at £2,650. Tenders were invited, but none was accepted at the meeting held in February 1900. This led to the abandonment of the plan involving the revestry site. Instead, it was agreed that a temporary song school should be set up above the slype in what was described as the lumber room next to the minor canons' vestry. By March 1900 that location was no longer a temporary expedient, for it was agreed that the new song school would take over the minor canons'

---

[14] 6 The College, now the Organist's house.
[15] G. W. Kitchin, *The Story of the Deanery, Durham* (1912), 53.

vestry as well, and that the work of converting the rooms would start at once. It was also decided that the old song school would become the new vestry for the minor canons and the King's Scholars, and that the adjacent music rooms would become a vestry and music room for the choristers.[16] The area selected for (and still serving as) the song school had housed the library in monastic times and later, and the minor canons had reached it from the spiral staircase leading to the central tower. A new access to it in the form of a wooden staircase in the slype, which was directly below, obviated the need for the boys to go into the cathedral.

The question of the boys' practice room had been settled, but where they should be taught had not. In March 1901 the working committee proposed that 'The Grove House', in Pimlico, should be adapted for the choristers. It was anticipated that there would be ten or twelve boarders, the rest being day boys. These proposals were rejected by Chapter later the same month, and the Grove House was handed over to Durham School.

For some years Meaden's health had been failing. In August 1887 a Mr J. Mowbray acted as schoolmaster, and in January 1896 George Ditchburn, one of the lay clerks, who had covered at the school in May 1895 when Meaden was ill, was appointed assistant master "during the pleasure of the Chapter". Ditchburn, however, did not stay long in Durham, for in December 1896 he resigned in order to become Master of the Choristers and a lay clerk at Manchester Cathedral. For five weeks in September and October 1900 a Mr [John] Fish deputized for Meaden.[17]

Early in January 1901 Meaden sought permission to retire, but agreed to continue until the Easter – and then continued until the summer, for in the July Chapter informed him that when he retired his pension would be £70 per annum. Also in January 1901 Chapter, appreciating that a resident assistant master would be a great help, appointed M. Gaston S. Harrison for the remainder of Meaden's headmastership. At the same time yet another sub-committee was appointed to report on the Choristers' School and the future.

It would be remiss not to say something about Philip Armes, who had succeeded Henshaw as Master of the Choristers on 1 January 1863. He has

---

[16] For more about the old song school and music rooms see p. **29**, n. **2**.
[17] Fish had recently retired from the Blue Coat School where he had been Headmaster since 1855.

been described as "a martinet and strict disciplinarian".[18] It was his wont to carry a military cane. This instrument he used both to administer punishment and for conducting. A musician of some distinction, he brought order to the music of the liturgy by arranging two sets of chants for the psalms.[19] He was also well to the fore in the re-kindling of interest in church music of the sixteenth and seventeenth centuries, and edited items from Durham's own music manuscripts of that period. It was his scheme for enabling internal students to study for the Degree of Bachelor of Music which the University of Durham accepted in 1886. The first group of music students, who gained their degrees 1891, included W. Liddle, a former chorister (1875-9). In 1897 Armes was appointed the University's first Professor of Music.

When Armes had been at Chichester the choir there had taken part in an annual Three Choirs' Festival with the choirs of Salisbury and Winchester. It was no doubt that Festival which prompted the choirs of Durham, Ripon, and York similarly to join forces. Their first joint Festal Evensong was held at York on 7 July 1881. The following year the choirs met in Durham. Several copies of the special service books containing the music sung at York on 27 June 1899 and on 3 July 1902 are in the Durham men's music library. In the 1970s, to increase the impact of the event, the service was moved from a weekday afternoon to a Saturday and there was an evening concert as well. In 1986 the occasion was expanded further by the inclusion of a sung Eucharist on the Friday evening, but in 1995 the choirs reverted to combining just for a festal evensong on a Saturday.

It is said that the choristers were present when the grave of St Cuthbert was opened in 1899, and that each was given a small piece of a wooden coffin as a memento. It was about this time, too, that Thomas Dixon (1897-1902) and Walter Laidler (1898-1903) managed to take some pipes from an old organ into town and blow them there. Unfortunately, they were seen by Philip Armes, the organist, and corporal punishment ensued.[20]

---

[18] C. K. Pattinson, "Cathedral Reminiscences" (1975), p. 1. Pattinson was a chorister, 1914-21, Bishop's chaplain, 1929-52, and precentor, 1948-72. His typescript is deposited in the Cathedral Library.

[19] See Music MS D12. Judging from later practice the first set (introduced in 1874 after an abortive attempt in 1863) was used during the odd-numbered months of the year, the second (introduced in 1876) during the even.

[20] Pattinson, "Reminiscences", pp. 2 (for coffin) and 1 (organ pipes).

1901-28: Dolphin and Dennett

On 20 July 1901 the committee proposed that minor canon A. R. Dolphin should take over Bennett's house [3 The College] when the latter's tenancy ceased on 23 November, and with it the care of the six boys living there; that Dolphin should be offered the position of Headmaster, and that £50 should be added to his minor canon's salary of £250 per annum.[21] It was intimated that Dolphin had been approached and that he was willing to accept these responsibilities. The proposals were approved, and it was also decided that there would be an assistant master and that his salary would be £80 per annum. In accepting Dolphin stated that he would marry at once so that he might have a capable Housekeeper!

Even before the formal approval of his appointment Dolphin had called on Harrison and expressed the hope that he would continue as assistant master. This reassured Harrison, who was neither a graduate nor a qualified teacher. Nevertheless he was concerned at the prospect of his income falling by £20 per annum. This led to negotiations with Chapter, and the undertaking that there would be no change to his salary.

Deliberations about the school continued, and Dolphin was approached for his thoughts on the enlargement of the school. He promptly consulted the Headmasters of the schools at Westminster Abbey, and at Gloucester, Lincoln, Salisbury and Winchester for advice about size and costs. Several of their replies advised him that the Durham costs would be greater because its choristers had far shorter holidays than theirs. The Abbey had five weeks in the summer and two at Christmas and Easter, and Salisbury had four in the summer, two at Christmas and one at Easter, where Durham had only a three-week break, and it was in the summer. That and the fact that as Dolphin had intimated there might be only six boarders led the Abbey Head to suggest that Dolphin would not be being unreasonable in suggesting the annual cost would be £40 per boy, and those at Gloucester and Salisbury to set the figure at £50. At £30 per boy the Lincoln Head claimed he was running at a loss, but this he was prepared to bear because the contacts he had made meant that another school which he owned was prospering and making a healthy profit.[22]

---

[21] Fate was doubly kind to Dolphin. Earlier in the year he had become a minor canon even though not he had not been short-listed for the position (Act Book for 6 April, 19 April and 1 June 1901).

[22] The scene at Lincoln, where the sixteen boys were sleeping two to a bed, left much to be desired.

As a result of his consultations Dolphin wrote to the Dean on 20 August 1901 stating that he was not in favour of other boys in the school. He gave the following reasons:

1. the boarding house and classrooms were inadequate for the 10 to 15 others boys needed to make the idea feasible; and there was no adjacent playground where the boys could relax in odd moments;
2. it was not clear how any non-choristers would spend the three hours each day when the choristers were at choir practices and services;
3. as there already were several good schools in Durham, he doubted whether 10 to 15 suitable boys could be attracted;
4. the fees to be charged should not be too low, otherwise the school might get the wrong class of boy. He suggested £45, with a £20 reduction for those who sang.

Dolphin's consultations and analysis were taken into consideration when on 16 November 1901 the sub-committee presented to Chapter the report it had assembled ten days earlier. It recommended that:

1. £250 a year for at least three years should be expended on running the house;
2. the Headmaster should be responsible for keeping the accounts and presenting them to Chapter;
3. £200 should be spent on furnishing the school as opposed to the Headmaster's quarters;
4. the boys' stipends of £20 and their leaving allowances should cease;
5. fees of £25 per annum should be charged for boarding and education;
6. the holidays should be increased to four weeks at least in the summer and two in the winter.

These recommendations were all accepted, and it was further decided that Harrison would continue as assistant master until 31 December 1902 at £2 per week.

Further recommendations formulated by the committee at its meeting on 27 January 1902 were accepted by Chapter on 1 February. These concerned making clear the terms on which choristers were accepted as boarders, that fees should be paid half-yearly in advance, and that there might be help from the Barrington Fund for the sons of clergy with livings in Durham and Northumberland. The holidays were to be as stated previously, and a list was to be drawn up by Dolphin of the chargeable extras – these were not to include surplices, sheets, or towels. The question of the remuneration to be made to a Matron, irrespective of whether she were the Headmaster's wife, was also considered; and the selection of choristers was entrusted to the Dean, Canon Kynaston, the Precentor, the Organist, and the Headmaster.

The decisions of January 1902 should not be taken as implying that boarding had become compulsory. This is made abundantly clear by a Minute of 15 October 1904, which resolved that advertisements for future Voice Trials should state that boys from a distance were expected to board.

Entries in the Act Book for 1902 to 1904 show Dolphin was allowed to do nothing of his own accord, only recommend. The decisions to buy new desks for the small classroom, to provide lockers and a table for the boarders, to allocate £5 from time to time for games for the boarders, to buy four large maps, a blackboard and an easel, to install a stove in the large classroom and gas brackets in the small one, and to fill in the saw pit in the joiners' yard so that that area might serve as a playground, were all made by Chapter.

Harrison's role as assistant master was appreciated, and successive extensions resulted in him continuing until 31 December 1904. Chapter even gave him permission, on 16 May 1903, to study for a Durham degree, subject to satisfactory arrangements at the school, and gave him £10 towards the expense involved. Later, it gave him a further £10 to enable him to move to Cheshire. On 1 January 1905 he was succeeded by D. A. Richardson, a graduate of Trinity College, Dublin. At £110 per annum his salary was the maximum Chapter was prepared to pay.[23]

In October 1905 Chapter started considering whether the recently vacant house attached to the First Canonry [4-5 The College] might be suitable for use by the school. Dolphin prepared costings based on 20 boarders plus himself, his wife, the assistant master and two servants, costings which re-directed the choristers' stipends towards their boarding and which included parental contributions. A positive conclusion was soon reached, and the work of conversion undertaken. In May 1906 the school, known as the Choristers' School to distinguish it physically from the song school, moved into the accommodation which was to serve it well for over forty years. The cost of the alterations had been limited to £500 plus the cost of installing electricity, and the cost of running the school, including salaries, was set at £1,150 per annum. The Headmaster's salary remained at £100 (in addition to what he received as a minor canon), his resident assistant's was set at £80.

---

[23] Harrison left in order to become ordained (see Minute for 19 January 1924). David A. Richardson, B.A., continued until 31 August 1906. He was followed by R. A. Cochrane, M.A., B.Litt. (1 Sept. 1906–[13] May 1908) and Hugh Pater (14 May 1908–1914). Pater, who had deputized during the inter-regnum, left in order to enlist, and was killed in action shortly afterwards. There are memorials in the Chapter House to those members of the school who were killed in the 1914-18 and 1939-45 wars.

On 20 October 1906 Chapter accepted J. Levesley's offer of a weekly Gym lesson. One should not conclude that the instruction begun in 1892 (see p. 53) had been discontinued at some point; rather this should be regarded as the moment when it was decided that the instruction should be throughout the year and not just a course lasting twelve weeks. Chapter also asked the Precentor, the Headmaster and the Assistant Organist to produce for the school a timetable like that being followed by the choristers of St Paul's Cathedral. What was probably the resultant timetable[24] is presented below in summary form:

Time	Routine (not Sundays)	Exceptions, &c
7.30 – 8.30 a.m.	Breakfast & Recreation	
8.30 – 9.00 a.m.	School	
9.00 – 9.45 a.m.	Choir Practice	Thurs: School
9.45 – 11 a.m.	Vestry and Cathedral	
11 a.m. – 12.50 p.m.	School	
1.05 – 1.40 p.m.	Dinner	
1.40 – 3 p.m.	Recreation	Tues: 2 – 3 p.m. Gym; Thurs: Holiday
3 – 3.45 p.m.	Choir Practice	Tues: 3.15 – 3.45 p.m. Choir Practice; Thurs: Holiday; Sat: Recreation
3.45 – 5 p.m.	Vestry and Cathedral	Thurs: Holiday
5 – 6 p.m.	Division I: School; Div II: Piano	Thurs: Holiday; Sat: 5 – 5.45 p.m. Choir Practice
6 – 6.45 p.m.	Tea and Recreation	
6.45 – 7.45 p.m.	Div I: Piano; Div II: School	
[8 p.m.	Bedtime]	

---

[24] It and copies of the Prospectuses mentioned below now form part of the Chorister School archive (see p. 53, n. 5).

The observations below the timetable included this analysis of the composition of the chorister's day:

Choir Practice, 1hr 30min nett; Cathedral & Vestry, 2hr 10min gross; School, 4hr 20min gross, 'as at S. Paul's'. 'Total per day 8 hrs. work + 2 hours fresh air (& Sunshine)'.

They also made it clear that the choristers had 13 days holiday after Christmas, 13 days after Easter, 29 days in July and August and 6 days in early October. It would be more correct to describe the first break as the winter holiday, for it did not start until the Monday after Epiphany (6 January).

Chapter continued to keep firm control of the school. Every month the Attendance Register and the Timetable were inspected at Chapter meetings; and an external examiner was appointed to report on the standard being achieved. If Dolphin wished to be away for family reasons permission had to be sought from Chapter and the names of the proposed deputies submitted for scrutiny. These included E. Kellett (one of the lay clerks), the Revd E. E. B. May, and on one occasion E. V. Stocks, the University Librarian, who was later appointed external examiner. In 1908 an area to the rear of the school was levelled to serve as a playground.

On 15 February 1908 it was decided that there was need for an Application Form. Comparison with the Prospectuses of 1906 and 1907 show that that for 1908 filled three sides instead of two, the Application Form occupying the fourth side. Further revisions were approved in 1911 and 1912. The latter edition showed that the school still numbered twenty boys, and included what was very much an outline of the daily routine given above. An examination of the outline confirms that the time spent on music was at least equal to that spent on school-work. The accompanying notes make it clear that Thursday afternoon, when it was Men's Voices at Evensong, really was a holiday, for, subject to satisfactory conduct, the boys were allowed home from 1.00 p.m. until 6.30 p.m. Such a statement, coupled with the fact that their train fare had to be enclosed with a written invitation, indicates that most of the boys must have been drawn from the north-east of England.

The notes in the 1912 Prospectus mention the summer, Easter and winter breaks, but give no indication of one in October. The earliest Attendance Register confirms that there was a 6-day break then from 1907 to 1911, but not thereafter. In 1912 and 1913 there was no break at all, in 1914 and 1915 a half-day, and a full day beginning in 1916. Even that must have come as a a half-day, and a full day beginning in 1916. Even that must have come as a welcome relief in a term lasting as long as nineteen weeks. The equivalent of Speech Day was held in the Chapter House shortly before the winter break.

The Prospectus then describes under "Extras" various financial and domestic arrangements. That about 'tuck' may cause surprise – but everyone was forewarned:

An account of the expenses incurred by the Headmaster on behalf of the boys, is sent in at the end of each half year (on or after December 25th and June 24th), and must be paid within ten days or an extra charge of 10s. is incurred. 25s. may be taken as the average for this half-yearly account. It includes Clothing and Tailor's repairs, boot-mending, Hair-cutting and Pocket-money. Parents are strongly urged not to supply their sons with an excessive amount of pocket-money. The Headmaster gives each boy an allowance of 2d. per week (monitors 3d.), and includes a charge of 2s. 6d. in payment for this item in the account at the end of each half-year. Any provisions boys may receive from home must be given to the Matron, and are dealt out at meal time for the benefit of the boys in common without respect to ownership. The Dean and Chapter bear the expenses of ordinary medical attendance and medicine during term time, but not Dentist's account. The boys' teeth are examined from time to time and a report is made upon their condition.

Boys on returning to School after vacation are required to produce a certificate that they have not been in contact with any infectious illness. [This was still happening in the 1960s.]

Finally, the Prospectus has a lengthy paragraph in which it extols the numerous physical and mental benefits resulting from being a chorister:

The constant reading of fresh music, with the part they play in the Cathedral services, is found to be a great factor in developing the Choristers' physical and mental powers. The chest and lungs are developed by the regular vocal exercise. In the hours devoted to music the boys not only learn elocution and voice production but they become acquainted through the Cathedral Services with the noblest English literature: their familiarity with the language of the Bible and Prayer book furnishes them unconsciously with a ready vocabulary of words and phrases for their English Compositions; and is found to be indirectly a considerable help to their reading and spelling. The eye is trained in alertness, the memory is exercised, and the accurate training of the ear is found to be of the utmost advantage to a boy when he comes to the study of a foreign language. Even from a purely commercial and practical point of view, the hours devoted to music are therefore by no means wasted; for regular practice in reading and rendering the works of the great composers (requiring as it does simultaneous attention to notes, words, time, and expression) is the best training a young boy can have in sensibility, concentration, accuracy, quickness, confidence, and intelligence. In other words, the powers called into vigorous exercise in the rendering of good classical music are those powers which make for success in after life.

Developments, however, were not confined to the academic scene. Minor Canon Bennett had assisted Armes with the choir and on the organ. When he fell ill early in 1901 lay clerks F. E. Leatham and W. F. M. Jackson were appointed to act as assistant organist and music teacher to the boys respectively, but on 2 November 1901 they were advised that their duties would cease at the end of the year. On 20 July 1903 it was agreed that there should be an assistant organist, at £100 per annum. Armes was instructed to choose a suitable person and to recommend him to Chapter. He selected William Ellis, of Richmond, Yorkshire, a former organ pupil.[25] Ellis's appointment, back-dated to 24 June 1903, was confirmed on 19 September 1903.

A meeting of Great Chapter, held on 1 December 1906, determined that on the resignation of Armes the position of Master of the Choristers should be offered subject to certain conditions to the Revd Arnold D. Culley, who, most unusually, was already the Precentor. Included in those conditions were: (1) that his duties as precentor and a minor canon were to come first; (2) that Dolphin was in charge of all school matters; (3) that an assistant would be needed, who would train the choir and play at services as approved by Chapter; ... and (7) that Ellis should be offered the assistant's position at £200 per annum. The decision to offer Culley the position was repeated when ordinary Chapter met on 2 March 1907. It was then also agreed that when Armes retired on 13 May 1907 he was to be given the title, 'Honorary Organist'. It was made clear that this title did not carry with it any duties, but was in recognition of his long and distinguished service. However, although Culley agreed to deputize as Master of the Choristers, the formal offer of the position was deferred more than once. It was eventually approved by Great Chapter on 20 November 1907, when it was decreed that his annual salary would be the statutory £10 together with an increment of £99. 4s. 0d. (i.e., a total of two guineas per week). That his

---

[25] For details of Ellis's career - he became organist of Newcastle cathedral in 1918 - see Watkins Shaw, *Succession of Organists*, 193. At Durham he was succeeded briefly by Basil Maine (Oct. 1918 to May 1919), and then by Cyril Maude who held the position until April 1967 – see pp. 73 and 82.

salary was lower than his assistant's and lower than the £210 received by Armes in his latter years was because of his other positions. For them he received £250 (as a minor canon) and £100 (as precentor).

Culley's musical pedigree was well established, for he had been Organ Scholar at Emmanuel College, Cambridge, but Armes, so it is said, was so upset that a clergyman had been appointed as his successor that he gave instructions that there was to be no music at his funeral.[26] A brass memorial to Armes is set in the west wall of the cloisters. It is rather sad to note that his widow had to be forbidden to clean it.[27]

In February 1914 Dolphin, who had accepted the living of Edmundbyers, was succeeded as a minor canon and headmaster by the Revd F. S. Dennett. At the same time the number of choristers and probationers was increased to twenty-four. Dennett was known to his pupils as 'Dammit', 'F.S.D.', and 'Freddie'. He is said to have ruled the school "with a rod of iron, or, if you prefer it, a selection of canes of different varieties and vintages".[28] He has also been described as a born teacher, with high standards particularly in Latin, French and English. It was, therefore, with some justification that Canon Fowler could write in 1915,

> The education is now modelled on that given in a good modern Preparatory School. The boys are taught Divinity, Latin, French, Algebra and Geometry, in addition to Arithmetic, and the usual English subjects.[29]

Under Dennett there continued to be only one assistant master. After several had come and gone in quick succession,[30] Tom Barton was appointed in September 1919. Apart from eight months in 1929 when he was Acting-Headmaster he continued in the position until his death in 1950. Barton, who had come out of the Navy in 1918, taught Mathematics and coached football and particularly cricket with great success. Nicknamed 'Pussy' – because of the spray when he spoke – he is remembered with great affection by those who passed through his hands. They tell how he kept the

---

[26] Reminiscence communicated by Norman[dy. A.] Lamidey (chorister, 1907-12).
[27] Act Book for 21 June and 24 October 1913.
[28] Pattinson also included these details in "The Precentor recalls ...", *The Chorister* (1963), 31-2.
[29] Fowler, "Durham Cathedral Choristers' School" (1915), 10-11.
[30] Those who acted for more than a month were: T. Job Davies (Oct. 1914–Jan. 1916), G. O. (Jan.–April 1916), L. R. Brown (May 1916–May 1917), E. MacLaren (May 1917–July 1918) and R. L. Marshall, M.A. (Sept. 1918–July 1919).

Potter's Bank field[31] like a bowling green. As well as the sporting activities looked after by Barton, the choristers had gym on Fridays in the Y.M.C.A. gymnasium in Claypath and from 1926 onwards swimming in a pool located in the basement of Bow School.[32] Both of these activities were supervised by Levesley.

There was also another, unofficial, assistant teacher – the Matron! On top of her many other duties as matron-housekeeper, Miss Frances Davis (1914-28) was given the responsibility of giving new boys a grounding in Latin and French. When Dennett became Rector of Shincliffe she followed him there as his housekeeper.

The interior of the song school
(reproduced from *The Cathedral Quarterly and Church Music Review*, iii, no. 9 (1915), p. 3)

In Culley's day the senior chorister was responsible for seeing that the choir maintained pitch, and for taking the boys' practice in the absence of

---

[31] It lost its rectangular shape when road improvements became necessary in 1946.

[32] The location had its drawbacks, and the pool was closed c.1940 (information from Mrs M. Adamson, widow of C. L. Adamson, Headmaster of Bow School, 1944-76).

the organist. As for the training of the choristers, much was passed on by the seniors to their juniors. This inculcation was assisted by the kicking of ankles. Culley accompanied practice principally with his left hand, emphasizing points as the occasion arose with the other, and joining in from time to time with a voice not unlike that of a corn-crake. He had a cane, but it was kept locked away in his desk. In Charles Pattinson's time (1914-21) it was brought out only twice and used but once. The stern look and the verbal rebuke were in themselves sufficient. Even humour had its grim note – for some years the first anthem after Culley's return from his summer break was "No chastening for the present", by Sullivan. As well as the music for services the boys learnt two oratorios a year, did vocal exercises, and studied music theory and harmony. They also learnt to play the piano or the organ or both, and had two half-hour lessons per week. It gave Pattinson no little satisfaction when, as Precentor, he lived in the house from which, by no means uniquely, he and his music had been propelled on more than one occasion.

From what their choristers say there was animosity between Dennett and Culley. They claim that Dennett was openly critical, but that Culley was more circumspect. Dennett, apparently, imagined that he could sing, and his penetrating attempts to do so irritated the organist and the choir. Culley forbade spare copies of the anthems and services to be given to Dennett. He reacted by buying his own. This led, it is said, to the decision by Chapter – it may have been informal – that only those who attended the full practice on Thursday mornings were permitted to sing. It is also said that Dennett, when a familiar hymn-tune was used to enable new words to be introduced, perversely sang the better-known words.

Kindly disposed towards the choristers was J. Meade Falkner, the author of *Moonfleet*. A director of Armstrong Whitworth, the Newcastle armaments firm, and also Honorary Reader in Palaeography at the University of Durham, he lived in Divinity House (now the University Music Department) on Palace Green. He used to entertain groups of choristers to tea on Sundays, present soloists with half-crowns, and 'reward' financially and with food the boys who delivered the weekly Service Sheets to his house.[33] To celebrate his marriage it is said that he transported his bride and all the choristers to Finchale Priory. There the boys played games, and enjoyed a delicious tea at a nearby farm.[34]

---

[33] Details taken from "'Wilkie' [Harold Wilkinson, 1911-15] looks back fifty years", *The Chorister* (1964), pp. 45-9, and Pattinson, "Reminiscences", p. 11.

[34] Memories of Thomas Dixon (chorister, 1897-1902).

Voice trials for boys' places in the choir were held from time to time. At that held in 1913 there were no fewer than 99 candidates.[35] The would-be choristers had to sing before Arnold Culley, the Precentor-Organist, their chief adjudicator, and several members of Chapter. The test was rigorous, with "scales up to top C, aural tests of some complexity; elementary theory; sight reading". It was an eliminating process, and the numbers were reduced to about 24. The boys then sang together in groups to see how they blended, and further testing took place after lunch. Eventually, those surviving all this were taken over to the school and subjected to some sort of academic assessment. Later in the afternoon the results were announced. The Minute of 15 December 1913 shows that nine choristers were selected. In the formal letter they received the parents of those chosen were advised that they would be contacted as vacancies arose through voices breaking. Once a boy's voice had broken, speed was of the essence. In most cases he would leave at once,[36] the Headmaster arranging for a school to take him if he were continuing his education. As for his replacement, it was not unusual for parents notified on a Tuesday to be asked to have their son ready to start at the school on the Friday of the same week.

At that time the usual attire was Norfolk suits and plain purple ties, with Eton suits worn on Sundays. The Eton suits had been introduced in the 1870s, apparently at the same time as the wearing of black cassocks during services. Previously the choir had robed only in surplices. The wearing of squares in the cloisters was approved in November 1879. The men's squares had black tassels, the boys' at first black and red, but later palatinate purple. Purple caps with a St Cuthbert's cross embroidered in gilt were agreed to in September 1901, the St Cuthbert's crosses worn in the choir by the senior choristers about the same time. Royal permission to wear purple cassocks was granted in 1933. Cloaks were still a thing of the future – they were not introduced until about 1964.

Some insight into a chorister's life c.1920 has been provided by Chris Abbey (chorister, 1915-21).[37] The youngest of five chorister brothers, he started singing with the choir during services even before he became a probationer. The four senior choristers were then known as 'corner boys'

---

[35] This paragraph is derived from Pattinson, "Reminiscences", pp. 2-3.

[36] Among exceptions who were allowed to continue their studies for a while were W. L. Everson, L. Forster, and G. C. Heyes (see Minutes of 2 Mar. 1912, 21 Apr. 1923 and 2 Apr. 1927). On 4 July 1931, early in Canon Ganderton's time, Joe Nicholson was granted an extra year at the school so that he could reach the matriculation standard required by Durham University.

[37] Christopher Abbey (*d* 1998) in conversation with me in 1997. I visited George Casey (mentioned at the end of the paragraph) in 1999.

because of where they sat in the choir. His third eldest brother, as No. 2 on Decani, was at the altar end of the stalls. Chris was instructed to sit across the gangway from him, and to move when the choir was singing so that he could share his brother's copy. He remembered playing football and cricket (there were school teams), taking part in athletics and going to the gym in Claypath. There was a Christmas Evening 'feed', and parties at the Deanery and in one of the canon's houses, but there were no Carol Services. He confirmed that L. R. Brown, E. MacLaren and R. L. Marshall were all assistant masters before Tom Barton; and that the boys were taught in two groups, with the assistant master taking the lower group. He remembered William Ellis and Cyril ('Pippy') Maude as assistant organists, Culley playing the 'Dead March' in *Saul*, and Dennett reading the Gospel on Christmas Morning. He was aware of the hostility between Dennett and Culley, and thought that Dennett was jealous because most of the boys liked Culley. Finally, he commented on Meade Falkner's financial generosity, not to himself but to Gavin Kay (chorister, 1911-18), who, because of his fine voice, regularly had solos to sing. George Casey (chorister, 1924-30) also recalled receiving 2s. 6d. from Falkner, but his was for delivering Service Sheets. He recollected swimming at Bow School – the basement was dark, its atmosphere unpleasant.

Two stories from those days have their humour. At that time the school had an 'isolation room' above the Chapter Office. Living in part of the building where the Chapter Clerk now lives was a Mrs Hodgson-Fowler, the widow of a former Cathedral Architect. In one of her frequent letters of complaint to the Headmaster she protested that when she stood on the lavatory seat in her house she could see boys running about naked in the isolation area![38] Again, when Alfred Phillipson (chorister, 1923-8) visited the school in 1993 he recalled how in the evening boys would fish for food from the dormitories, the 'catch' being attached to their lines by the maids.

In January 1929 Dennett accepted the living of Shincliffe. As his successor at the school was not available until the September, Barton was appointed 'Acting-Headmaster'. During this interregnum Dennett was required to do some teaching, and appointed to assist Barton was a Mr J. Grome Merrilees.

---

[38] Pattinson, "Reminiscences", pp. 29-30.

7. Wider Horizons

1929-57: Conformity and Expansion

Like his two predecessors, the Revd H. Y. Ganderton ('Gandy') was a minor canon as well as Headmaster. Like them, this resulted in his minor canon's salary being increased initially from £250 to £350 per annum. Unlike them, he was familiar with the academic scene, for he had been on the staff of St John's College, Durham, since 1920, and its vice-principal since 1924.[1] As a result he appreciated that certain aspects of the structure and role of the Choristers' School needed changing to enable the education being imparted to be more effective. Those aspects are stated time and time again in his Speech Day Reports, beginning with that for 1929, delivered at the end of his first term as Headmaster.[2]

He stated then that he was very aware that he was building on foundations laid by others, and he spoke about examinations. They were, he said, "a useful incentive to work", for they provided

1. a test of the work done – the amount of ground covered and the standard reached,
2. a means of selection for a prize or scholarship, and
3. a test of the school or system (when considered in the light of the external examiner's report).

He congratulated those who had won prizes, but had more to say to those who had not. They should not be content to drift along, but should set themselves high targets. As for the prizes, he pointed out that the work done during the year and other factors had had to be taken into consideration as well as performance in the exams. This was because

there is not much competition in so small a school as this, where the ages and capacities of the boys differ so widely.

With education becoming more and more important, he was pleased to inform parents that two of the three leavers were going on to Durham School, and he urged the parents of the others to start making similar

---

[1] His association with St John's had begun in 1912 as an undergraduate. His contribution there is appraised in *The Johnian* (1929), 23-4.

[2] When he became Headmaster the school's year had its peculiarities. It began in late January, about a fortnight after the end of the previous one. Speech Day was held at or near the end of the academic year. Only in 1951 was the start of the school year moved to September. His Speech Day Reports were published privately by him in *The Chorister School* (*c.*1968).

arrangements for their sons. He made it clear that he regarded the Choristers' School as a Preparatory School, albeit a Preparatory School with limiting features. Not only was it important to go on to the next stage and increase one's knowledge, but moving on to a larger school – and starting again from the bottom – would knock any conceit out of them and round off any sharp corners.

But although schoolwork was clearly important, so too was a balanced routine. To that end, he reported, he had already made some minor modifications to the school day, with the result that there was "more time in the open air for their games". He expressed himself to be "a great believer in fresh air and exercise for growing boys", and stated that, with the boys' work in the cathedral, song school, and the classroom all indoors, it was his objective

> to give them at least one hour's exercise in the open air every day -
> on the playing field when possible, otherwise by a run, a paper-chase
> or a walk.

He reported on the winner of the Gym Cup and gave news of recent Old Boys. He probably surprised parents when he said that "as an old friend of the school" he was well aware of the hard work done over the years for the school and the boys by Dennett, Barton and Miss Davis (the former Matron). Justification for him describing himself in such terms has been found in the Chapter Minutes for May and June 1922. From them it transpires that Chapter accepted his offer to provide a closed Scholarship (of £40 a year for three years) to a former chorister going on to St John's College. It seems likely that the beneficiary was Charles Pattinson (who had gone on to Durham School), for in December that year Chapter granted him a £40 a year scholarship at Durham University, and he went to St John's.[3]

The size of the school was commented on again in 1930, Ganderton observing that there were

> special limitations involved in a small school such as this, where the
> boys are divided into two forms only: Seniors, whose ages vary from
> 12-16, and Juniors from 9-12. In many subjects the forms are sub-
> divided into two or more divisions.

This time he did not comment on the limited competition. Instead, he pointed out that a small staff meant a limited curriculum. The absence of Science from it was placing boys at a disadvantage when they progressed to their next school. In 1933 he reported that two demonstrations involving

---

[3] 'Patter' later became Bishop's chaplain, precentor, and a master at the school.

simple experiments had been given by one the University lecturers, though they were not a satisfactory alternative to regular lessons.

In 1930 Ganderton also remarked that the unpredictability of the moment of transfer to a boy's next school presented problems too. This was because it did not take place at a certain age, but only when the boy's voice had broken. As some schools had waiting lists he advised parents to try to anticipate the event by making provisional arrangements. Some years later, in 1938, he observed with some satisfaction that there was only one boy aged fifteen in the school (and he was leaving), where in the past sixteen and even seventeen year olds had not been uncommon.

On other matters he was able to report in 1930 that Palmer's Close had become available for football, thus allowing the Potter's Bank field (not then affected by the roundabout) to be in good condition for the cricket season. He commented that there had been an Athletic Sports Day in the Easter Term, and that a Junior Gym Cup had been promised by Dr Crawhall.

1932 saw the long nineteen-week 'Christmas' term reduced by two weeks – a week had been added to the end of the summer holiday, and the Christmas holiday had been moved a week earlier. Ganderton then went on to say that with boys joining the school whenever older boys' voices broke there was no effective beginning or end to the school year. Two boys, he said, had started the school at the beginning of the Christmas term, and two were starting the following term. As the first two had had seventeen weeks of Latin and French and had made progress, they could hardly go back to the beginning – so their group would have to be sub-divided. Continual divisions of this nature meant that setting an exam for the whole of a group was proving far from easy.

Ganderton may have been a minor canon and played his part in services, but that did not restrict his vision. In 1933 he had this to say:

> In the curriculum of a Choir School music must of necessity hold an important place, and perhaps crowd out other admirable subjects. I hope it may never assume such proportions as to be detrimental to the general education of the choristers.

Having so said, he proceeded to analyse how a boy's day was spent, and expressed his opinion in such a way as to invite the Dean & Chapter to consider the matter further. He told the gathering,

> Every day of the week at least three hours are taken up with the music practice and Choral Services, on some days more than that. When you consider that 5½ hours is the normal working day of a boy in a day school, it appears to be a matter of serious concern whether the proportion be not too large.

In June 1937 he no doubt thought the opportunity to increase the size of the school, and with it the numbers of members of staff, had arrived. Aware that Bow School, a similar-sized Durham preparatory school, was up for sale, he wrote to the Dean & Chapter suggesting that the two schools should be merged. Later in June Chapter decided against any action for the present,[4] and in December 1937 Bow School was acquired by Miss M. M. Lodge, who had previously taught at Durham School.

That Ganderton had long been sound in his opinions was confirmed by the national review of education which took place in the mid 1940s and which led to the 1944 Education Act. In the summer of 1943 the Choir Schools' Association discussed the implications of the proposals for secondary education, and later that year Ganderton applied for the school to be recognized by the Ministry of Education. It was also in 1943 that the Dean & Chapter, aware of the increasing importance of the 'School Certificate' as a preliminary qualification, resolved that due regard had to be paid to safe-guarding a boy's future. Accordingly, it decided that, irrespective of whether his voice had broken, a boy could leave when he had reached the age of fourteen, and that in normal circumstances he must leave by the end of the term in which he reached his fifteenth birthday.

A preliminary inspection of the school took place in July 1944, and various issues were discussed with the Inspectorate. In his 1944 Report Ganderton commented on the recent Act: "New schools are projected, to be equipped in a manner undreamed of in the past, the school leaving age is to be raised, better training is to be provided for teachers, and increased pay, and so on", but "there is one notable omission" – "parents should provide better boys, and possibly better girls – I don't know about that!" This he expanded by saying, "I maintain the home is the natural teacher of the child in his earliest years. It is there he should learn the first principles of good behaviour and right conduct ...."

He then informed parents that one change had already been implemented, for Science was now in the senior form's curriculum. It was being taught by Dr Gibby,[5] who had been allowed to use the facilities at Durham School. Other changes, too, were under discussion; and he prepared parents for these by saying:

---

[4] He was not the first to have plans about Bow School. As a result of a proposal made the month before by H. K. Luce (Headmaster, Durham School) Chapter was awaiting information about Bow's finances.

[5] The 1941 Report mentions that Science had been introduced for some senior boys, and Chorister Account Book 2 confirms that Dr C. W. Gibby started then. He continued in a part-time capacity until his retirement in 1967.

I have for a long time felt that the choristers would benefit education-
ally if the present number could be increased by the inclusion of a
proportion of non-choristers, without changing the essential character
of the school as a Choir School. Such expansion would make it possible to group the boys more effectively according to age, encourage
more competitive work among them, give them the advantage of a
larger teaching staff, and the benefit of a common life with more
varied interests and experiences to share.

Early in 1945 the formal inspection took place. Its report could have
been written by Ganderton himself, for it found that:

1. the great disparity of age among the boys created special difficulties
   in such a small school;
2. too much of the boys' time is spent in their musical training
   [Ganderton reckoned about 20 hours per week were spent on
   cathedral practices and services], which has the effect of crowding
   out other important educational activities such as handicrafts, nature
   study and art, and giving the boys too little leisure in which to pursue
   activities of their own choice;
3. the age at which the choristers left to go on to other schools was too
   high.

Ganderton included these criticisms in his 1945 Report. In response to
them he reminded parents of the proposal to expand the school, and he
added that he also wondered whether the hours spent on the boys' musical
training might be reduced "perhaps by having only one practice on a day
when there is only one choral service",[6] and whether the age at which the
boys left should be reduced from 14+ to 13+.

In 1946 Ganderton stated that the expansion of the school had been
delayed for a year or two. This was because it depended on the buildings in
The College being used by St Mary's College becoming available. When it
became apparent that it would take the University some years to provide a
new College, Chapter decided to proceed with the expansion. Its plan to
introduce a few non-choristers at Easter 1948 was postponed for one term
when it learned that Mrs Evelyn Blyth[7] would not be available until the start

---

[6] It must be remembered that at that time Matins was still being sung on Tuesdays
and Thursdays.

[7] Alderman of Durham, and in 1954-5 its Mayor. Her brothers, Harry and Fred
Smurthwaite, had become choristers in the 1910s. While she was Mayor, Adrian
Officer, F.R.S.A., took her form until Christmas 1954. The Revd L. G. W.
Russell (from Fourah Bay, Sierra Leone) then filled a temporary vacancy until
July 1955.

of the normal academic year. Then, in September 1948, four day-boys and eight boarders were admitted, making a total of 36 boys in the school.[8]

There was not really room in the existing buildings for this increase. The kitchen could not cope, and arrangements were made for the extra boys to eat at lunch time at the Victory café then located in Saddler Street.[9]

The existing two-form structure, with more than one age-group in each form, was not equipped to accommodate the extra boys either. This situation, coupled with the fact that the choristers then still had cathedral duties from 2 p.m. to 4 p.m., explained why Mrs Blyth had been recruited, for during the first term of expansion the non-choristers were taught by her as a separate group. After that, three integrated age-based forms were set up, but these functioned only on certain mornings.[10] This undesirable state of affairs, with the non-chorister group increasing in age-range as well as in size, continued until January 1952, when the time of Evensong was moved from 3 p.m. to 3.45 p.m., with practice held afterwards and not before. 3.45 p.m. was not as late as Ganderton had hoped – in 1948 and again in 1949 he had indicated that he was in favour of 5.00 or even 5.15 p.m. In 1949 he also said that pressure from parents meant that he had reduced the entrance age for 'non-choristers' from nine to eight.

'Ma' Blyth's 'bark' had an electrifying effect on the boys. This was apparent to other members of staff and later to John Grove [Ganderton's successor], for they too were met with the instinctive "Yes, Mrs Blyth!" when they issued stern commands. On one occasion, when a small boy claimed he was doing nothing, she expressed the opinion that he must be an ornament and promptly put him in what she considered an appropriate place – on the mantelpiece! On another occasion, she picked up a howling new day-boy who was unwilling to leave his mother and carried him into the school – he later became a 1st XV stalwart.[11] Long after her retirement in 1959 former pupils still spoke of the occasion when she stepped backwards into the pond during a rehearsal of an open-air school play.

---

8   The termly fees at that time appear to have been about £10 (for choristers), £17 (day boys) and £45 (boarders). The uncertainty is because with the levying of fees then retrospective, the inclusion of 'Extras' obscures the basic amounts.

9   Information from Alan Terry, one of the 1948 intake, after he had opened the Nursery department on 10 October 2008.

10   The non-choristers had a broader timetable – it included Art and Handicraft lessons (taught by Mrs MacFarlane-Grieve and then by Miss Peddlesden) and Nature Study. Their involvement and later details about members of staff are confirmed by payments in The Chorister School Account Books.

11   The boys were Rory Hannah (1958-63, mantelpiece) and David Pickering (1957-62, day-boy).

In 1950 Tom Barton died after 31 years at the school. In view of his great love of cricket and the way he had coached the boys the Dean & Chapter presented the school with the Barton Memorial Cup. This is still awarded each year to the best cricketer. Appointed at Easter 1950 to replace Barton as teacher of the middle form was a Mr Craven. On the boarding side he seems to have been replaced first by 'Paddy' Smythe and then by Euan Curtis.[12] Also involved with the School were Dr Gibby (who had been teaching Science since 1941), Canon Charles Pattinson (the former chorister who had been appointed Precentor in 1948) and Dean Alington, who continued to give a weekly Poetry lesson in the Deanery. The 1950 Speech Day was the last to be held at the end of the Christmas Term. Some nineteen months elapsed before that for the year 1951-2 was held in July 1952.

In July 1952 parents were asked to ensure that their sons conformed to the standard dress of the school. This was stated to be: "medium grey suits in the winter, and grey flannels in the Summer (shorts to be worn unless permission has been obtained to wear long trousers), together with the regulation school cap, tie and stockings. A school blazer is also a desirable addition."

In September 1952, when Mr Francis[13] joined the staff, there were 63 boys on the books. Nos 4-5 were no longer large enough, but delays in the University's building programme continued to hold up both the proposed move and further expansion. For some time a spare room in what was the Bishop of Jarrow's house (No. 15) had served as an additional classroom. To this was now added the wooden building at the bottom of the garden of St Mary's College. It had been the College chapel; its future role would be a games and hobbies room. Building delays were not the only frustration – the levelling of Palmer's Close, the re-turfing of its centre, and the re-routing of a footpath across it, all needed putting in hand.

---

[12] A Mr Phillips, a retired teacher, deputized in 1949 when Barton became ill. Arthur Craven continued until August 1951. B. H. Smythe (May 1950–Easter 1953) was resident and taught some History while studying for his Diploma in Theology at St Chad's. Curtis (Sept. 1953–Aug. 1957) was a History graduate of St Andrews. He taught Algebra, Arithmetic and History, and played the bassoon. In cricket practices he used his hockey stick to direct the ball to fielders. He left to teach in Glasgow. 'Patter' taught English and Geography, and later, French. He took the 'non-chorister' groups for music – and introduced them to the delights of Gilbert and Sullivan. Various others, including students, helped for short periods.

[13] A graduate of University College, Durham, Humphrey C. H. Francis, M.A. (*b* 1889, *d* 1971) had been a boy at Haileybury (1904-7). Latterly he had taught at Newbury Grammar School (1940-52). At one time an area co-ordinator for the St John Ambulance Brigade, he was still an active member.

It was only at Easter 1953 that the school was able to take over the house which had been used by St Mary's College, in the south-west corner of The College.[14] Even so, it still had the use of the highest two floors of No. 5. Everyone was struck by the fact that the rooms in the new building were much lighter.

Numbers continued to rise, the hundred being reached in September 1955, and further staff were recruited.[15] Much to their surprise they found that, even though there were enough of them resident to share out the duties, they were all expected to make the school their lives and be on duty with the Headmaster every evening. They also found that even the 'new school' was not large enough, and in September 1955 the room recently vacated by the Cathedral Architect on the top floor of the Chapter Office became a classroom.

Keeping pace with the increase in numbers was an academic interest and awareness. This was demonstrated in two spheres: on the one hand, there were successes in the Common Entrance and Scholarship Examinations to Public Schools; and on the other, the school, now known as The Chorister School, was inspected during the Easter Term 1957 by the Ministry of Education and recognized as efficient.

As a distinct enlarged existence had been preferred to merging into Durham School, from 1944 onwards Conrad Eden, the Organist, found his role somewhat altered. It looked as if he and his successors would be training boys only to lose many of them before their most useful period.[16] Moreover, as a firm commitment had been given to expand the school by accepting boys other than choristers, cathedral duties would no longer be the only consideration in determining the daily routine.

Eden, who had come from Wells in 1936, was not Culley's immediate successor. That had been [Sir] John Dykes Bower, who had been appointed in 1933. The latter's pleasant manner had delighted both men and boys; and they thought his stay had been far too brief when, in 1936, he became Organist at St Paul's, London. It was in June 1933, shortly after Dykes Bower's arrival, that Chapter obtained permission from King George V for

---

[14] It was officially opened by Lord Lambton at Speech Day 1953.

[15] Alan Oyston, B.A. (Sept. 1955–Aug. 1956; former chorister; St John's Coll., Cambridge), D. Stuart Halder, B.A. (Sept. 1955–Aug. 1964; former chorister; University Coll., Durham) and Kenneth J. Edge (Sept. 1956–Aug. 1966; alto lay clerk to Aug. 1964).

[16] With the generally earlier onset of adolescence this has not been true of the scene since 1980. Quite a number of boys have ceased singing treble before their thirteenth birthday.

the choir to wear purple cassocks instead of black ones. The Minute records that the actual shade was to be determined by the canons' wives!

When war was declared Chapter allowed those parents who wished to do so to withdraw their sons. As a result, between September 1939 and the end of 1940 there were no fewer than eleven new boys. Eden was called up, and saw active service in India. While he was away Cyril Maude, who had been the Assistant Organist since 1919, took charge of the choir. As a result, there were choristers who received their entire musical training from him, and thought of him as 'the Master of the Choristers'.[17] When Eden returned after the war and found that some of the senior choristers were using physical force to transmit their knowledge to their juniors, he was appalled. He pointed out to them that it was unacceptable aggression which had caused the recent conflict and cost many their lives.

But even before Britain declared war, the school had become aware of the effect of Nazi anti-Semitism. On 31 December 1938 Canon Ganderton obtained permisssion from the Dean & Chapter to bring to the school one or two of the "'Non-Aryan' Refugee Boys" who were then arriving in Britain. He wasted no time. Early in January 1939 he went to the refugee camp at Dovercourt, near Harwich, and chose, in very much the same way that one would choose a pet from a pet shop, George, a young Jew from the German Baltic port of Stettin.[18]

George was aged 11½ when he arrived in Durham in the middle of January 1939. Only ten days had elapsed since his parents had secured for him a place on one of the *Kindertransport* then leaving Germany. His English was very limited when he arrived, but within a year he was attending the same lessons as the other boys. Later he won a prize for English. Like the others he knew the chapel in the Deanery undercroft as both a dormitory and an air-raid shelter.[19]

---

[17] His title on the Service Sheets is 'Sub-Organist'. He could not even be described as 'Acting Master of the Choristers' because he covered during what was 'an extended leave of absence', not an interregnum.

[18] Contact between George Bendori (*d* 2007; formerly Rechelman) and his contemporaries was re-established in 1996 after a break of over 50 years. Most of what follows about him is selected from the letters he wrote in response to my many questions. For an edited version of his first letter to me see *Friends of Durham Cathedral, 64th Annual Report, 1997*, 25-30.

[19] Prior to it becoming such in 1940 the choristers had had to leave their dormitories for the basement of 6 The College whenever there was an air-raid warning.

The Deanery Chapel as a dormitory cum air-raid shelter

Like the choristers he wore an Eton suit on Sundays and special occasions. He did not sing in the choir,[20] but he did attend Sunday Services and Carol Services. He also remembered Christmas with its presents and legal pillow-fight, and the party at the Deanery. Sharing in the life of the choristers of an Anglican cathedral was not the culture shock that one might suppose, for many German families only learnt to their cost of their Jewish ancestry through the Nazis checking back several generations.

On Thursday mornings, when the choristers had Matins followed by 'Long Practice', George was allowed into town. There, in the days before rationing was introduced, he acted as a messenger for the other boys, buying sweets and other items for them. At other times he was permitted to go sculling on the river. Assigned to his special care was the garden of the 'Count's House'.[21] Because he was not a chorister it was never his duty to collect daisies for Dean Alington to chew! He remembered playing table-tennis, and also being allowed to play with Ganderton's train lay-out which was on a specially constructed table. On one occasion he played with it without permission, caused a major derailment and fled into town.

It was not only George's generation which was woken by the call: "Wakey, wakey, rise and shine, you've had your time. Heave out, heave out, lash up and stow. Shake a leg and make your bed."[22] These instructions, to get out of one's hammock and ensure that it was not an obstruction, Ganderton and Barton themselves had heard when they served in the Royal Navy.

Peter Allsop remembered the wartime dormitory in the Deanery undercroft as a rather creepy place. He recalled how one night a normally locked adjacent area was found unlocked. The boys, being inquisitive, investigated, and soon afterwards some of the seniors were indulging in a couple of bottles of wine which they jealously guarded from the juniors. Although they looked, they never found that area unlocked again.

When Allsop was at the school food rationing was still in operation. Regarded as treats were scraping out the milk pudding tin at the end of the

---

[20] George was not the first 'non-chorister' – on 1 October 1921 Chapter had agreed to Canon Dolphin's son attending as an "extra to the choir".

[21] The 'Count's House' had been fitted out as a Carpentry shop in 1933. In late 1934 and early 1935 Mr Hollis (a Dean & Chapter workman) taught the boys there.

[22] This fuller version - I had previously heard the central sentence from a number of sources – was communicated to me by Peter Allsop (1944-7). Contact with him was re-established as a result of his sister (a former St Mary's student) visiting the school in 1999 during her college's centenary celebrations.

meals and eating the toast left by the staff. In contrast the Christmas dinner was a rather splendid meal, and the serving of the pudding was preceded by "a noisy interlude of spoons hammering on the dinner table." The Matron (Tom Barton's wife) used the relevant coupons to buy an assortment of sweets. These she sold to the boys twice a week. "Typically you got half a bar (1 oz.) of Blended chocolate, 5 Black Bullets, or a similar quantity of other goodies she had in store. Price in each case I think was 2d. which was marked down in a record for settlement at a later date. (We weren't allowed to have cash except if we had to go to town to buy something, and permission to do that was rarely given.) Most of us tried hard to find ways of making these sweets last as long as possible. I'm sure one of us must have originated the idea for a 'Flake' bar because one of the ways to prolong the chocolate was to shave the bar with a pen-knife and eat one flake at a time."

As well as the Matron there was "a cook, two or three maids, and Boots, a man who looked after all our footwear and no doubt had other duties."[23] Among other things that Allsop wrote about were the twice-weekly baths in one of the three baths. That the bath water had to be shared was put down to the shortage of water and the lack of fuel to heat it. [Only after an extra boiler and more cylinders had been installed some time after 1978 did it prove possible for each boy to start with clean hot water.] Cricket and soccer were played depending on the season, but rugby was not – black eyes would have been unseemly on cathedral choirboys!

Several former pupils have also mentioned Ganderton having a startling reminder of his war experiences at the Battle of Jutland.[24] It happened when a blank cartridge, which had somehow found its way into the classroom fire, exploded behind him. Others remember well April Fool's Day, when for a while they were allowed to play tricks on him. Even trip wires and notices incorporating 'anser-ton' [a Latinized version of 'Gander-ton'] brought no rebuke.

1957-78: Academic prowess

In September 1957 the School may have had a history stretching back over 540 years, but in its last nine years it had undergone a dramatic trans-

---

[23] Those other duties included looking after the coke-fired boiler. I remember it well – until it was converted to take gas I looked after it at weekends and often checked it last thing at night.

[24] He published privately his own account of that battle in *The Battle of Jutland* (n.d.), itself an offprint of part of his *Under the White Ensign* (n.d.).

formation.[25] It had grown from a closed community of twenty-four boys to an open one of over one hundred. The time was therefore ripe for developing further strengths. Though the list is not his, nor does its order indicate priority, it would seem reasonable to suggest that the Revd John M. Grove,[26] the new Headmaster, set himself thee targets:

1. to fuse the three separate elements [choristers, other boarders, and day boys] into one effective unit;
2. to establish high academic standards; and
3. to improve the school's facilities.

An early step in the fusing process was the allocation of the boys into four houses named after the Bishops Flambard, Langley, Pudsey,[27] and Skirlaw. Each House had its share of the three elements, and it was the opinion of the established members of staff, after the initial allocation had been made, that all the 'rogues' of the school had ended up not inappropriately in Flambard, with the author as House Tutor.[28] At that time Flambard was not one of those included in the cathedral's Service of Commemoration of Founders and Benefactors, but when this was pointed out to Dean Wild an appropriate clause was added. Certainly, the House system gave the boys a strong sense of belonging, a spirit evident in the inter-House competitions for work and behaviour and for sport.[29]

The integration was promoted further by the introduction of a number of out-of-school activities. To the Cub pack started under Canon Ganderton was added a Scout Troop. Both groups were run enthusiastically by Ken Edge, who was assisted by students at the University. Local activities were

---

[25] 1957 marks the beginning of the author's association with the school. Although this section and the next are based on his own memories, due regard has been paid to Canon Grove's *The Chorister School, Durham, 1957-1978* (1980), and to his and Mr Lawrence's Speech Day notes and the School Magazines.

[26] Hereafter he is referred to as Canon Grove, even though it was not until 1974 that he was made an Honorary Canon.

[27] The form 'Pudsey' is now recognised as a corruption of 'Le Puiset'.

[28] Under William II Ranulf Flambard (bishop, 1099-1128) was keeper of the king's seal and the instigator of unpopular financial policies. A suitable scapegoat, he was imprisoned by Henry I, but became the first person to escape from the Tower of London. He sided with Robert of Normandy in his claim to the English crown, but escaped punishment when Robert ceded to Henry.

[29] Right at the outset Dean Wild presented a Cup for work and behaviour; another was provided for Athletics; and leavers presented Cups for Rugby (Richard Baron), Cricket (Peter Cavey) and for Swimming (Thomas Muir).

participated in, and camps were held in England, Scotland, Wales, and Guernsey.[30]

On Thursdays many day boys stayed for tea at school so that they could attend the Debating Society run by Cyril Watson.[31] This was partly because they were captivated by his 'dramatic' History lessons. At the Debates there was a boy chairman, boys were the main speakers, and all boys were encouraged to speak from the floor. From time to time there were also Mock Elections. For that in March 1966 Tony Blair (day boy, 1961-6; Labour Prime Minister, 1997-2007) stood as the *Conservative* candidate. It must, however, be pointed out that by the time of the final speeches on the eve of polling day illness had overtaken him. He was replaced by Richard Stewart, who was duly 'elected'. 'Blair 2' (as he was known) also achieved fame by writing 'rhinoceros' as an answer in a Maths test. When asked why he had done so, he replied that he knew that the name for the longest side of a right-angled triangle was something like 'hippopotamus'!

Even more binding than the House system – and rewarding in other ways too – were the School Plays. From humble beginnings in the school's dining room and in the gym of the High School for Girls (then in Leazes Place under Miss Fenton) they progressed to elaborate productions in the University's Assembly Rooms. Cyril Watson, their producer, seemed to devote every spare moment to going over words and rehearsing movements. He was expert at type-casting – he it was who cast Rowan Atkinson (boarder then day boy, 1964-8) as the eccentric Dauphin in Shaw's *St Joan* – but he also cultivated stage presence by having young boys as pages and older ones

---

[30] The total cost (train fares and ferry charges included) of the 1963 camp on Guernsey for 47 boys and adults was just over £500.

[31] Assistant Master, 1957-64 and 1966-94. He acquired the nickname 'Clag' as a result of objecting in a Carpentry Club session to a boy using that word instead of 'glue'. This incident was referred to (not entirely correctly) by James Fenton in "Of cathedrals, class and clag" (*Independent* for 16 January 1995). For many years Mr Watson had boarding responsibilities. One night, after midnight, he woke up to find two boys and a policeman in his room. The boys had been found over a mile away from the school, and the policeman felt he ought to return them to someone in authority. As he did not wish to climb back out over the wall the dressing-gowned Mr Watson had to take him down The College and let him out.

as soldiers and the like. When he did have a rest year, others maintained his high standard.[32]

Also playing an important part in the integration process were the School Services held monthly on Sunday mornings in the Galilee Chapel. Introduced by Mr Grove *c.*1960, they regularly attracted over a hundred parents and boys. The Galilee choir, which led the singing at these services, included the cathedral probationers. Some years later it was directed by Maurice Armsby (teacher and lay clerk), and acquitted itself well in a series of 'Epilogues' on ITV.

And yet, in spite of the integration and the passage of time, there were choristers in the 1960s who, unaware of the past, preferred the sessions in early September, at Christmas, at Easter and at the end of the summer term when there were only the choristers in the school. Various immediate reasons were given for this. Among these were: the outings to York and the Farne Islands; the festivities of the Christmas period even though term did not end until the Sunday after Christmas; the uplifting music at Christmas and Easter; and the fact that only in the early September session were there any lessons, and then only in the mornings. For those giving the matter more thought, it transpired that the choir was the unit to which they felt they really belonged, and they appreciated the fact that in those sessions their day was timetabled round what was musically required of them.

With respect to his target of high academic standards, Canon Grove felt that if suitably qualified teachers were to be attracted then their salaries should not be inferior to those paid by the state sector.[33] The yearly budget must have been carefully costed, for the basic termly fees in 1957-8 were: choristers £28, boarders £62 and day-boys £31.

That high academic standards were indeed achieved may be gathered from the number of scholarships and exhibitions gained to Public Schools: 129 awards at 29 different schools in 21 years. The striving for excellence may have been given undue prominence, but its effect was far-reaching, for nearly all the boys who sat the Common Entrance Examination took it in their stride, only eleven failing to reach the school of their first choice.

---

[32] His other productions included: *Adventure Story* (Rattigan), *Androcles and the Lion* (Shaw), *Becket* (Anouilh), *Caesar and Cleopatra* (Shaw), *Gunpowder* (Margaret Till), *Richard of Bordeaux* (Daviot) and *The Royal Hunt of the Sun* (Shaffer). Other members of staff produced *Julius Caesar* (Shakespeare), *Joseph and the Amazing Technicolor Dreamcoat* (music by Lloyd-Webber), *Noye's Fludde* (music by Britten) and *Toad of Toad Hall* (Milne).

[33] As a new teacher straight out of College in 1957, I started at £625 p.a.

These successes were due partly to the quality of the intake, partly because in the higher forms subject specialization was preferred to class teaching, and partly because changes in staff were few.

In 1957, Thursdays excepted, the choristers had choir practices every morning from 9 a.m. to 10 a.m. Matins was sung on Tuesday and Thursday mornings, followed on Thursdays by 'Long Practice' until lunch time. It fell to the Head Chorister to take the last half hour of this practice.[34] All of this meant that the school day had to be carefully planned. As a result only one games afternoon was possible, and the choristers missed out on class Music lessons and had to have their swimming sessions together (and not with their forms) on Friday evenings after tea. Moreover, it proved impossible for the choristers in the senior forms to have any Art at all. When weekday Matins was phased out in April 1970, these divisive aspects disappeared, and, though the time the choristers spent in school increased, a more balanced timetable was achieved.

Rugby was introduced into the school, but only occasionally was there a really good team – such things call for more than one session per week, and for playing together over a number of years rather than just in one's final year. Cricket, on the other hand, was more successful, with the school producing numerous fast bowlers in the early 1960s. At athletics the school had its own system of 'standards'. Introduced in 1958, long before the '5-Star Award' scheme, it encouraged every boy to focus on the events which appealed to him. That the overall standard was good was evident when the school began to take part in the mid 1970s in the area meetings organized by Red House School, Norton.

Science had been taught mainly at Durham School to the top form only. In advance of the subject being included in the Common Entrance Examination a laboratory was set up above the Chapter Office in 1967, and Science was taught to the top three years. Then at Easter 1970 the school acquired the lower two floors of 10 The College[35], which had become vacant through the retirement of the Ven. J. O. Cobham, the Archdeacon of Durham. The rooms it provided meant that there was a special room for Morning Assembly, that the Library was no longer a few shelves in a classroom, and that the boarders' Common Room was no longer a classroom during the school day. No. 5, where the school had been since 1906, no longer housed any classrooms or staff accommodation (though the Scouts

---

[34] The Head Chorister was also busy at unaccompanied Evensong on Fridays. After the service he had to report any deviations in pitch to the organist, who already knew because he had been listening from behind a pillar in the Nave.

[35] The '9' still on the door in 2008 denotes the building's former number.

and Cubs used the top floor for a few years more), but the Science laboratory and one classroom were still above the Chapter Office.[36]

The provision of a music block in 11 The College meant that the choristers could all have their instrumental practices on home ground. No longer had they to go to the Deanery (and converse with the Dean as they passed through the breakfast area!), the houses of the Organist, the Chapter Clerk and some of the Canons, and the remote boys' vestry. For most of his time as Master of the Choristers Conrad Eden gave piano lessons to all the choristers, and also brass, string, and woodwind lessons to a few who took up a second instrument. After Bruce Cash became Sub-Organist in 1968 some piano lessons were delegated to him; and when Alan Price, a violin teacher, was appointed a bass lay clerk in 1970 he was invited to take over those learning that instrument. When Alan Thurlow[37] succeeded Bruce Cash in 1973 he became the school's Director of Music as well. This led to the recruitment of other specialist teachers.

1970 also witnessed the first step in moving later the time of Evensong. It was hoped the move would make it easier for those who aspired to be lay clerks to find the other employment needed to give them a reasonable salary. The change effected in the April, from 3.45 to 4.00 p.m., however, was little more than tinkering, though it did enable each of the three short afternoon lessons to be extended by five minutes.

Not long before he retired Canon Grove was also consulted about a possible second change in the time. He built up evening programmes for the school with Evensong at different times, and concluded that the later the time of Evensong the shorter the free time the choristers would have each day. Although it looked as if the change had been shelved, it later transpired that it had only been put on hold.

1975 witnessed the end of the Eton suits the choristers had worn on Sundays and the starched collars they had worn at every service. The school had been told that the collars were no longer obtainable, though it later transpired that other choirs were still able to get them. The boys were probably not sorry to see them go, for they had chafed many a neck, and the stud holes quickly became too large, rendering the studs ineffective. No longer did the boys have to wear shirts with detachable collars: they too

---

[36] It was in that classroom in 1963 that John (now Jon) Bell succeeded in knocking himself out: in his eagerness to get his Maths book marked he forgot that the teacher's desk was on a dais.

[37] He left in 1980 to become Organist at Chichester Cathedral, a position from which he retired in 2008.

could remove their ties and undo the top button on warm days or when playing in the yard.

The last physical change was in 1976, when it was decided to connect internally the school and No. 10. The intervening old stables and hayloft were converted into a classroom and Art Room respectively. The latter may be thought to be very lacking in natural light, but the original plan was for the Library to be there.

Among events which happened in Canon Grove's time undoubtedly the most memorable took place in 1967. That was when the cathedral was the setting for the visit of the Queen on Maundy Thursday to distribute the Royal Maundy Money. Those who were choristers then will remember the boys of the Chapel Royal staying at the school. They wore their distinctive red and gold outfits for the service, but their buckled shoes were not quite what they seemed – the buckles were on thick black elastic which the boys slipped over their shoes. The Durham choristers received two payments for the part they played in the service: a television fee, and a set of silver Maundy coins. One boarder also received a set of coins: he was David Bailes. He had the honour of being one of the posy-carrying Children of Charity who traditionally accompany the Queen on this occasion.

Also memorable was a day in 1974. The choir found out before Evensong that after the service it would be taken to Newcastle to sing "Ave verum corpus" (Dvorak) on TV. It transpired that Archbishop Ramsey (formerly a Canon Professor and later Bishop of Durham) had announced his retirement, and that London wanted the Durham choir to sing his favourite anthem. The bus driver got lost (twice), and when the choir arrived the programme had already started. There was just time to be told where to stand and to practise the anthem once. Much to producer Mike Neville's surprise the choir did the latter unconducted while he explained to Richard Lloyd (the Organist) the precise timing of the choir's contribution.

One other event happened quite regularly until 1967, when Choral Communion became a weekly instead of a monthly Sunday service. Major Nicholson used to come in from Plawsworth by horse-drawn coach to Matins. After the service he would invite choristers to ride on top of the coach. They were taken over Prebends' Bridge, up to the White Gates, and along to Durham School. From there they walked (or ran) back to school.

8. Wider still and wider

1978-94: Further strengths

In appointing Commander Raymond Lawrence, a Housemaster and Head of Geography at Taunton School, the Dean & Chapter introduced a man who had considerable experience and who was capable of helping what was still a fledgling school into soaring flight.

Where in the past a boy's position in his form[38] had been determined by the addition of marks scored in examinations and monthly orders, it was now felt more appropriate to give grades not only for achievement but for effort as well. This encouraged all boys, whatever their ability, to give of their best, and at the same time it removed some of the pressure from the more able, for it was no longer important to be in 'the top three' in a class.

This did not result in a falling away from the high standard achieved in what may be described as the academic subjects. The reduction in the number of lessons allocated to Latin, Mathematics and English in the senior forms,[39] did not affect it either. As a result, more creativity and balance was brought into the timetable, for it became possible for all members of every form to have Art lessons.

In this more creative climate, and under David Hill, who had succeeded Alan Thurlow as Sub-Organist and Director of Music, there was something of an explosion in the number of boys learning musical instruments. Music was no longer the preserve of the choristers and a few other boys – it was quickly developing into one of the strengths of the school. Whilst, choristers excepted, a boy did not have to be musical to come to the school, it was agreed that every opportunity would be taken to develop whatever musical abilities he might have.

When in 1985 David Hill moved on, the decision was taken to appoint a Director of Music who had no cathedral responsibilities. That Director was Jennifer Openshaw (later, Tasker), one of the visiting music teachers. Music became timetabled for every form. The lessons were used not just for singing but for the theory of music as well. Musical assessments were made, and boys showing that they had the aptitude were encouraged to take up musical instruments. In 1992-3, when there were about 160 boys at the

---

[38] This is its turn affected where they sat in the dining hall and their prospects of receiving second helpings.

[39] Latin and Mathematics had at one point been allocated seven lessons each.

school, no fewer than 130 individual lessons, many given by visiting music teachers, had to be fitted into the weekly timetable. Many of those making good progress on their instruments entered the appropriate age-group of the internal annual Michael James music competition.[40] A small orchestra was established, and often half its members were not choristers.

The school choir, which had previously functioned mainly at the School Services, flourished. It began to feature at public concerts[41] and other functions in its own right. Occasionally it sang Evensong in the cathedral when the cathedral choir had commitments in the diocese. It also started combining with the choristers for the School Carol Service and End of Term Services, and for the performance of a substantial work[42] each year, the lower parts being sung by friends of the school. The effect of all this music-making was that Music Scholarships and Exhibitions were won by day boys and ordinary boarders as well as by choristers.

It also proved possible to introduce a second 'games afternoon'.[43] This meant that some time could be given regularly to developing skills, rather than one match being the preparation for the next. It was also decided that for rugby and cricket there should be more than just one School team. Second teams came into being, and so did Under 11 and Under 10 sides. As a result the standard in these sports improved considerably, not least because it meant that boys were playing together at a competitive level for four and sometimes five years rather than just in their last year or two. At swimming the school began to feature prominently in area meetings, and at athletics a number of boys reached the national finals. The sporting area also witnessed one other change. First Richard Lloyd, who had succeeded Conrad Eden as Master of the Choristers in 1974, and then James Lancelot, who followed him in 1985, occasionally permitted a number of choristers to miss practices and services in order to represent the school.

---

[40] This was first held in 1989-90. Michael James had no direct connection with the school. A former Organ Scholar of University College, Durham, he died while waiting to take up an appointment as Assistant Organist at Rochester Cathedral. The Chorister School is one of the beneficiaries of the Trust Fund established in his memory.

[41] For some years it has been the choir giving the Christmas Carol Concert in one the Durham churches in aid of The Children's Society.

[42] For instance, Britten's 'St Nicolas', Duruflé's 'Requiem', Fauré's 'Requiem', Haydn's 'Nelson Mass', Mozart's 'Vesperae solennes', Purcell's 'Dido and Aeneas', Rossini's 'Petite messe solonnelle' and Stainer's 'Crucifixion'.

[43] Or rather, re-introduce. That scenario had prevailed temporarily while the under-floor heating was being installed in the cathedral (November 1966 – May 1968) and Evensong had been at 4.45 p.m. For some of that time weekday Matins was held in the very cold Galilee chapel.

Such co-operation would have been difficult before 1978, for until then either the Master of the Choristers or the Headmaster had overlapped with one of those who had been in those positions when the school widened its horizons in 1948. Now in charge were people both of whom appreciated that as each had responsibilities for the choristers they should work together. As a result meetings were set up so that they could determine together how the demands of future events on the boys should be met. Under Raymond Lawrence and Richard Lloyd the meetings were not held on a regular basis, but they became weekly when James Lancelot succeeded Richard Lloyd. Once the position of Boarding House Master had been created, he participated as well.

It has already been mentioned that during Canon Grove's headmastership nothing came of the second attempt to alter the time of Evensong. The idea was resurrected in 1979, and in September that year Evensong was moved from 4.00 to 5.00 p.m., and finally in September 1984 to 5.15 p.m. Interestingly, these later times would have been welcomed by Canon Ganderton in the late 1940s (see p. 79). Although Canon Grove had not been mistaken when he concluded that the block of free time between tea and prep would be eroded, there was now time for the choristers to unwind between the end of school and going over to the cathedral. Also, instead of there being an anti-climactic practice after Evensong it became possible to have a meaningful one before the service.

Also changed was the time of the morning choir practice. This had long been held from 9.00 to 10.00 am, but this meant that the rest of the school was holding its assemblies and temporising at a time when the young brain was probably at its sharpest. Yes, two hymn practices a week meant that there was an extensive repertoire of hymns which were sung well, but valuable teaching time was being lost. When Mr Lawrence approached Richard Lloyd about this he found that the idea of an earlier practice accorded with his plans too. As a result the practice was moved half an hour earlier.

Changes there were, too, to the buildings and their furnishings. The acquisition of the top floor of No. 10 meant that a number of subject class-rooms could be located there, thereby enabling the Science Laboratory above the Chapter Office and the Second Form to be transferred to the ground floor of No. 10. The new classrooms, and in time the old ones, the dormitories, the staircases and most of the corridors were all carpeted. This had the effect of reducing the noise level as well as creating a more homely atmosphere. In the classrooms desks were replaced by tables, and blackboards and chalk by whiteboards and marker pens; and television sets and computers began to find their way into classrooms. In the dining room the old wooden tables and their linen tablecloths, the benches and chairs were replaced by formica-topped tables and benches. The old ones were in a state of collapse, and the new tables had the advantage that they could be dismantled, though they did have one drawback: they did not absorb the noise in the way the wooden ones had done. The facilities were further improved when the dormitories were equipped with new beds and lockers. The basements were modernized and extended by enclosing the space under the verandah, and the three totally inadequate showers, which dated back to the 1950s, were replaced by a more realistic number.

Even more noticeable among the physical changes was the provision of a Sports Hall in place of the wooden hut which had originally served as St Mary's College chapel. The Sports Hall was opened on 21 September 1987 by Colin Moynihan, the Minister for Sport.[44] At the same time the yard was extended, though plans for a larger play area were somewhat thwarted by the planners insisting that the pond, which dated from the early 1700s, be restored where it was.

Changes also took place on the boarding side. Where in Canon Grove's time 'Exeats' had been limited to part of a number of Sundays each term, the national attitude to boarding was changing. Mr Lawrence was quick to appreciate this and offered weekly boarding. As a result, and very much against the national trend, there was at times a waiting list on the boarding side.[45] The weekly boarders went home at lunch-time on Saturday and returned on either Sunday evening or Monday morning. In view of this the choristers, too, were allowed more 'freedom'. Those who lived near enough were able to stay at home on Sunday evenings throughout the year, and on Saturday evenings during the Summer Term and the first half of the Michaelmas Term. Leave was also granted on Thursdays between 'prep' and 8 p.m. These changes may have suited 'the customers', but as a result some felt that the boarding side had lost its identity as a community.

---

[44] That was in the afternoon. In the morning, in a different capacity, he had taken part in the ceremony which had launched the Cathedral and Castle as one of England's first World Heritage sites.

[45] Parents of many senior boys responded to the suggestion that it was easier for their sons to adjust to boarding at a school with which they were familiar than be faced with that additional challenge when they moved on to their next school.

The school grounds in July 1973

The ability to attract boarders and day boys was also helped in July 1992 when an agreement was entered into with the trustees managing the funds which had accrued from the sale of the site of the former Rosebank School, Hartlepool. As a result The Chorister School was able to use some of the annual income from the fund to assist parents living particularly in the Hartlepool area with the school fees.

For some years Mr Lawrence pressed for the addition of a pre-prep section open to both boys and girls. He felt that this was necessary to ensure the future of the school, especially as the parents of prospective pupils were starting to commit themselves to a rival establishment which had such a section. A start was eventually made in September 1992 when a spare room in the school became the classroom for a group of seven six-year-old boys.[46] During that academic year much of the ground floor of 12 The College was converted to house the new department which would take boys from the age of four. These new premises were opened by Tony Blair, M.P.,[47] on 22 October 1993.

Where in the early nineteenth century Maria Hackett had campaigned for the better education and general care of the choristers, now concern was being increasingly expressed by the teaching staff about the length of the choristers' day. Over the years the time spent in class had increased, and the amount of time spent in the cathedral was certainly not less than it had been when the Inspectors had commented on it in 1945 (see p. 78). For some boys, for whom early morning sessions were the only way to accommodate all their instrumental practices, there was scarcely any respite between getting up at 6.50 a.m. and going for showers at 8.15 p.m. One member of staff (Geoffrey Howell) remarked somewhat wryly, "The trouble with the choristers is that they are always supposed to be somewhere else five minutes ago!" One suggestion made from within advocated a reduction in the length of the morning practice, but the decision taken by Chapter following a visit by two HMIs was to abandon Boys' Voices Evensong on Mondays. This gave a block of free time on that evening matching that on Thursdays.

---

[46] They were taught by Miss Jo Thoy, who was later appointed Head of the pre-prep department, a position she still [2008] still holds.

[47] At that time a newly elected member of the Labour Party Shadow Cabinet; see also p. 87.

Their busy working day was also offset by longer holidays. There were other compensations, too, in the form of the first choir tour, recordings, and high-profile services including broadcast and televised services. Nor must the visit to London in May 1981 to take part in St Paul's Cathedral in the 327th Annual Service for The Corporation of the Sons of the Clergy[48] be overlooked. All the way back Richard Lloyd was concerned whether the train would make an unscheduled, but privately arranged, stop at Durham. It did.

The last significant change was in the role of the Headmaster. Where Canon Grove had managed to attend to the school's correspondence, answer the telephone and teach over thirty periods of Latin to five classes, the increased demands of administration, meetings and recruiting meant that as the years progressed Mr Lawrence found a regular teaching routine was no longer practicable. As he needed to be easily available throughout the day, a small study accessible only through a classroom or eerie back stairs was no longer practicable. A more appropriate room was chosen, and to enable the school to be run efficiently secretaries were introduced. As well as teaching Geography the Headmaster's wife, herself an able teacher, acted as bursar and oversaw the boarding side. On the teaching side, Mr Lawrence appointed a Director of Studies. Finally, in 1990, he became the first Headmaster since the beginning of the century not to be resident and directly in charge of the choristers and boarders. As no member of staff was leaving in the summer I agreed to take over looking after the boarders, with a qualified Matron and a gap-year student to assist me.

1994-2002: Co-Education

By retiring at Easter 1994, and not in the summer, Mr Lawrence enabled his successor the more quickly to introduce his own policies. When the pre-prep department was launched in 1992 the admission of girls had been mooted, but the decision had been delayed. Mr Stephen Drew, the new Headmaster, was suitably experienced to implement such a development for he had come from Rugby School, where with his wife he had been a tradition-maker, setting up a girls' boarding house. At his first Speech Day, in July 1994, he was able to announce that the policy to admit girls had been agreed upon. It

---

[48] A few men and boys had also taken part in May 1978 in the service marking the 300th anniversary of this charity being granted a Royal Charter. In May 1997 the whole choir went down again. This time the travel plans were straightforward.

would be executed in stages beginning in September 1995 with the admission of girls to the pre-prep department, but in the meanwhile 'guinea-pigs' would be welcome.[49] It was, however, stated that no decision had been made whether girls might offer themselves as choristers, that this was an area where there were many factors to consider.

The first intake of boys and girls was split into two classes under Miss Jo Thoy and Miss Laura Riberzani. Each class embraced more than one age group, both were located on the ground floor of No. 12. One of them overlooked the river, the other was in the room that had been the house's kitchen. With its medieval central column and arched vault, the latter was certainly an unusual location. The second intake was similarly divided, but the third enabled the three different age groups to be taught in separate classes. By September 1998 there were over 50 children in the pre-prep department. Taught sometimes in five classes, sometimes in six, they occupied the whole ground floor of No. 12.

The creation of the pre-prep department not only offered a service to parents, it also served to generate a more substantial intake into the First Form (Year 3).

The fact that the early admissions of girls were limited to the pre-prep department gave the school time to provide the facilities required by the co-education of children aged eight to thirteen. First and foremost were the provision of separate toilets and separate changing and showering areas in the basements; and what might be described as the east wing was identified as suitable for this conversion. It also proved suitable for the location of a girls' dormitory once sufficient girls had reached an appropriate age, and for accommodation for a female gap-year student to look after them. Prior to the creation of the dormitory Canon W. N. Stock and his wife provided sleeping accommodation for the first girl boarder[50] – her brother was a chorister, and she herself was musical. By 2002 girl day boys and boarders accounted for about 30% of the school; and in 2001-2 in Kimberley Forrest they provided their first Head of School.

It should be mentioned that when they were still at the junior end of the school, the girls joined in sport with the boys, and Kimberley proved good enough to play rugger for one of the junior sides. Much to the consternation of her opponents – who would still be musing, "Isn't that a girl?" – she would gather a pass and leave them standing. The appointment of a girls' games teacher soon resulted in the introduction of girls' games instead. This

---

[49] There was one such 'guinea-pig' in September 1994: Victoria Lawrence, the daughter of the previous Headmaster.

[50] Kate Telfer, the sister of Jack.

99

was an important factor in turning what had started as a boys' school with girls in it into a properly co-ed school.

Another important change was the re-location of the Headmaster's office and those of his secretaries. Instead of being hidden away in the remote recesses of the boarding end of the school, they were moved so that they were immediately accessible inside the much more impressive entrance to No. 10. This had the further advantage of placing them at the heart of the main teaching block.

Other room alterations included the relocation of the kitchen into what had been a large room given over to washing up. This function was transferred to the smaller adjacent room which had served at times as a small dining room and as a rest room for domestic staff. What had been the kitchen became the Technology Centre, the base for a subject which was beginning to play an important part in the curriculum.

A different sort of change of location was the setting for Speech Day. Previously the speeches had been made and the prizes distributed in the ballroom on the lowest floor of Dunelm House. An interval then followed to allow people to walk the quarter of a mile or so to the cathedral for a service. Up to 1984 that service was the normal cathedral evensong, but in 1985 the service was held with the school very much in mind. In 1999 the two parts were combined and held in the cathedral. The Headmaster's address and prize-giving were followed by a specially devised simple service in which the pupils led the prayers and a few hymns were sung. Providing sufficient seating was no longer a problem, and as a dais under the central tower was the focal point even those sitting well back could recognise the prize-winners.

Although the morning practice had for some years taken place between 8.30 and 9.30 a.m. it was felt that this still intruded too much into the teaching day. As a result, in about 1994 the start of the morning practice was moved to 8.10 a.m., and the practice itself shortened so that it ended at 8.55 a.m. This enabled lessons to begin at 9.15 a.m. The loss of practice time was redressed by second practices held in the school Assembly Hall. At first these were on Wednesdays from 12.15 to 12.45 p.m., and then one on Fridays was added. Later, the second practice on Fridays was dropped.[51]

---

[51] This may well have been a consequence of no school on Saturdays. It has not been established when the timing of the second practice on Wednesdays was altered to 1.15 to 1.45 p.m.

These changes, however, were minor compared with the ending in 2001 of school on Saturday mornings. It was a development needed to keep the school on an equal footing with its competitors. It was welcomed by the parents of day pupils, who were spared doing two double journeys in such a short space of time; and it enabled day pupils and boarders alike to spend more 'quality-time' with their parents. With a practice on Saturday morning, and practice and a service on Saturday afternoon, the choristers had to remain at school, but there was a gentler start to the day, and time for an instrumental practice as well as time to relax.

The awareness of what was happening elsewhere had resulted as early as 1995 in the choristers finishing a night earlier at Christmas. Previously they had gone home after breakfast on Boxing Day, but it was felt that there was little point in this when so many of the chorister parents came to Evensong on Christmas Day so that they could see their sons. It made much more sense for them to go home after that service.

Christmas and Easter services and broadcasts did not provide the only musical excitement for the choristers, for there were tours in 1996 to Denmark, in 1998 to Norway and in 2000 to both Germany and far off Brazil. That to Brazil took place 4-15 December, and was at the invitation of Cultura Inglesa.

Nor was music just the preserve of the choristers. Music throughout the school continued to flourish, and the Michael James competition to appeal to ever-increasing numbers. The School Choir continued to flourish, with the annual Children's Society Carol Concert one of its highlights. Even more notable was its appearance on 28 March 1998 at the Stadium of Light (the ground of Sunderland AFC) where in the entertainment before the match it sang an item composed by Julian Stewart-Lindsay. Later it gave the first performance of his 'Vox Dei' at a millennium concert held in the cathedral and featuring performances and performers from Tyneside and Wearside.

Something must also be said about the school's dramatic productions. In 1994 Stuart Otley produced three open-air performances of 'The Tempest' by Shakespeare by the whole school, but thereafter his efforts were devoted to performances by his own form, the First Form. Two other productions would not have taken place had it not been for the Headmaster. In 1998 he adapted 'Pudding and Pie' from *Dobsons Drie Bobbes*, a book published in 1607 about a Durham chorister in the 1560s (see pp. 20-1), and purloined the music for his song lyrics from *The Beggar's Opera*. A similar adaptation and borrowing of music from more recent popular shows took place in 2001 for *Man of Steel*, which was based on the superman story. This combination of talents the Headmaster had displayed some years earlier at Speech Day 1994, when as part of the farewell to the long-serving Cyril Watson he wrote his own verses to Sir Joseph Porter's song from *HMS Pinafore*,[52] and performed them with various other members of staff and the School Choir.

Success in a variety of spheres helps greatly to persuade parents to send their children to a school. This was not just left to word of mouth or newspaper reports, but Open Mornings were held so that parents and, just as importantly, their offspring could experience the atmosphere that the school generates.

This 'at-home' side of recruitment was complemented on 1 July 2002 by the inauguration of an Outreach Programme. Planned by Canon Lancelot,[53] Mr Drew and Mr Stephen Auster (the Head of the Music Services for Sunderland's Education Department), it involved a number of choristers visiting the Benedict Biscop and Richard Avenue Primary Schools and making music with the pupils there. This was an important first step, and more will be said later about the programme.

As a result of these various initiatives the school continued to grow so that the total number of pupils hovered round the 200 mark. More importantly, when Mr Drew left for pastures new in 2002 he had transformed in just over eight years what had been a boys' school into an integrated co-educational establishment.

The present and the future

The appointment of Ian Hawksby marked a new departure, for although he had no experience of private education and boarding schools, as the Headmaster of a Church of England Aided School he was familiar with developments in the state sector and experienced in the sphere of co-education.

Since his appointment the girls have become a force to be reckoned with, gaining scholarships and exhibitions to their next schools. At sport some of them have represented the county and the region for their own age-group and for the one above. Within the school they have had their share of prefects, and in 2003-4 and 2006-7 provided the Head of School.

---

[52] I was presented with an acrostic sonnet to mark my own retirement in 1996.

[53] In recognition of his contribution to music in the diocese as well as in the cathedral, James Lancelot, the Organist, had been created a non-residentiary Canon by the Bishop.

Recent years have seen the school excelling at Design Technology and Information Technology. Gary Brown, the master in charge, has become the Incorporated Association of Preparatory Schools' national co-ordinator for those subjects, and has run courses not only at a national level but in conjunction with Durham University as well.

Northumbria University has recognised the school as a suitable establishment at which would-be teachers could receive their training. Lin Lawrence devised the courses of study, and John Keys and Mo Brown became accredited tutors. Ian Hawksby himself has been appointed an Independent Schools Inspector and is a member of the Choir Schools' Association National Committee and Working Party.

From its humble beginnings in July 2002 the Outreach Programme has gone from strength to strength. The links formed with the Sunderland schools have continued, and in 2003 eight schools there were visited during the Easter and Michaelmas terms.

The pattern is for two schools to be visited in one morning. The schools are told something about the musical history of the cathedral, the choristers sing to the pupils, who then sing to them, and finally both groups sing together. The programme shows the children at those schools, some of which have very limited musical facilities, 'that the cathedral is there for all the region, that music goes on in there every day, that boys need not be embarrassed about singing, that children can sing to a high standard, and that even only a few voices can fill a large space if they are well trained and developed. Above all, ... that singing is a natural activity which humans being have engaged in for thousands of years'.

The contact does not end with the visits to the schools, for also in the Michaelmas term thirty children from each school are invited to come to the cathedral for a music workshop and concert. Nor is it just the children who come, for their parents and friends come too and fill the building. As well as encouraging the children to make music, the programme does have an ulterior motive, for it is hoped that there might be something of a return, 'that suitably gifted boys might be moved to try for the cathedral choir.' [54]

New links have now been forged in Middlesbrough, and contact is now going to be extended to schools in Durham County and Tyneside. This co-operation between the private and state sectors is encouraged and supported by the government, a support which brings financial benefits to the school. Other benefits are manifest in the recruitment of two choristers and in the

---

[54] Information drawn from James Lancelot, "The Outreach Singing Programme" (*Friends of Durham Cathedral, 70th Annual Report, 2003,* 36-38).

formation in 2007 of the Durham Cathedral Young Singers, a group which has already featured in concerts both locally and in Newcastle.

The success of the Outreach Programme owes much to the continuing co-operation between the Headmaster and Canon Lancelot. This was particularly apparent during the 2005-6 season when the 1st XV gained a National Award for winning all its ten games and scoring 486 points with none against. The five most senior boys in the choir and two other choristers were key members of the team. They were allowed to miss a number of practices, though they were required to be at services. The success of the attempt to get them to the cathedral on time owed much to the fact that long cassocks provided an ample covering for dirty knees! The picture has been painted of a chorister bearing down formidably on the wing, and then an hour or so later singing a heart-rending treble solo.

A musical highlight took place in June 2008, when a French tour saw the cathedral choir sing in Notre Dame, Paris, the cathedrals of Chartres and Versailles, and in two other French towns. But again music is not just the preserve of choristers. Wherever there is musical ability every attempt is made to foster it; and entries for the recent Michael James competition had to be limited in order that all could be heard in one evening. It should also be mentioned that the pre-prep recently showed that it was in no way inferior when it came to music-making.

It might be thought that with all these strengths the school can afford to rest on its laurels. Not so: it must continue to attract pupils by persuading parents to commit their children to it at any early age. With this in mind September 2008 has already seen the opening of a Nursery taking children from the age of three. The term has also seen two voice trials for a completely new departure:[55] the creation of a second 'top line' for the cathedral choir. The hope is that, beginning in September 2009, there will be twenty girls of comparable age to the boys. Like the boys they will board at the school. Each team will provide the top line at four services each week; and the prospect of them combining on certain occasions is even more exciting.

---

[55] It was claimed in the *News in Brief column* in the *Musical News and Herald* for 9 February that 'at Durham Cathedral, for the first time, the applicants for choristerships include three girls'. [News item resurrected by Alan Gibbs in *Organists' Review*, May 1995, p. 92, after the initiatives led by Salisbury and Warwick to introduce girls' voices.] The cathedral archives shed no light on the situation; and certainly, prior to 2008, no girl has ever been elected.

Supporters of the English choral tradition will also be heartened by the probable return of sung Evensong on Mondays.[56]

These developments are prudent, and should ensure the School a successful future. Though change for change's sake is both unsettling and frustrating, yet at the same time change is growth. Merely to maintain the *status quo* is to stagnate, and to stagnate is to die. Worthwhile elements should be preserved, but the target should always be to improve. That the last 80 years have been placed under the headings "Wider Horizons" and "Wider still and wider" is testimony to the fact that the Governors have appointed a succession of five Headmasters who wished to add to the school's strengths. That is why a small school which was exclusively for the cathedral's boy choristers has developed into a thriving Preparatory School for boys and girls. Long may the School prosper!

---

[56] See p. 97.

Instructors in Music

1387-8	NICHOLAS the Cantor (*possibly*)
1415-16	Dom WILLIAM KIBBLESWORTH (*d* 1416-17)

Secular Cantors[57]

1416-17	WILLIAM CHANTOUR
1418-22	RICHARD WYMOND
1423-4	HUGH WESTMORELAND
1424-6	WILLIAM DAVY
1430-87	JOHN STELE (contracts, 22 Dec 1430 & 2 Jan 1448; *d* 1487)
1487-96	ALEXANDER BELL (Informator, New Coll, Oxford, 1485-6; Informator, Magdalen Coll, Oxf, 1486-7; Durham, contract, 23 June 1487; mr of chors, Salisbury, 1496-1502)
1496-1501	THOMAS FODERLEY (contract, 23 June 1496)
1501-6	JOHN TILDESLEY (contract, 23 June 1502)
1506-12	ROBERT LANGFORTH
1512	ROBERT PERROT (of Magdalen Coll, Oxf; Durham contract, 28 Apr 1512, rendered void because continued at Magdalen; the Durham contract refers to him as PORRET)
[1512-13	WILLIAM ROBSON (in temp capacity)]
1513-25	THOMAS ASHWELL (*b c.*1478; Informator, Lincoln, 1506-13; Durham contract, 24 Dec 1513)
1527-34	WILLIAM ROBSON (in his own right; *d* 1534)
1535-9	JOHN BRYMLEY (*b c.*1502; contract, 17 Feb 1537)

Masters of the Choristers and Organists

1540-76	JOHN BRYMLEY (*d* 13 Oct 1576, aged 74)
1576-88	WILLIAM BROWNE, 20 Nov 1576–Sep 1588, see under 1599 for 2nd spell (chor, ←Sep 1566–20 Nov 1576)

---

[57] Special abbreviations: ← = before, → = after, adm = admitted, app = appointed, assist = assistant, can = canon, chor = chorister, hon = honorary, lay cl = lay clerk, min = minor, mr = master, org = organ / organist, prec = precentor, prin = principal, ret = retired, resig = resigned, superintend = superintendent, supernum = supernumerary, Xtmas = Christmas

1588-9   ROBERT MAYSTERMAN, Sep 1588–c.Jun 1589 (b c.1546; chor, ←1557-67; lay cl, 1577–death; d of "the plage"; *bur* 20 Sep 1589)

1589-98   WILLIAM SMYTHE, Mar 1589–Sep 1598→ (b c.1553; chor, 1564-70; min can, 1576-1600; *bur* 21 Jan 1604)

1599-1607 WILLIAM BROWNE, again, ←Sep 1599–Sep 1607→; (?org, York, 1607-16)

1608-1612 EDWARD SMYTH, ←21 Oct 1608–death (*bap* 5 Mar 1587; chor, 1597-1601; *bur* 4 Feb 1612)

1612-13   [FRANCIS] DODSHON, for "about a year and a half"–Sep 1613 (*bap* 7 Mar 1568; chor, 1580-4; lay cl, ←1612-17; org, Southwell, 1617–death; *bur* 7 Dec 1622)

1613-46   RICHARD HUCHINSON, c.Sep 1613–May 1628, when reduced to org only[58] (*bap* 4 Oct 1590; chor, 1601-7→; d 7 Jun 1646)

1628-33→ HENRY PALMER, mr of chor only, 7 May 1628–Dec 1633–? death (lay cl, 1627–d 29 Dec 1640)

1660   two unnamed masters of choristers, simultaneously

1660-77   JOHN FOSTER, Xtmas 1660–d 20 Apr 1677 (chor, ←1630-8→)

1677-81   ALEXANDER SHAW, org only, June 1677–expelled Xtmas 1681 (chor, 1661–sackbut; sackbut player, 1664-72; ?org, Ripon, early 1677; *bur* 23 Jul 1706)

1677-81   JOHN NICHOLLS, mr of chors only, Jun 1677–death (chor, 1637→; lay cl, 1660–death; mr of Langley song sch, 1667–death; *bur* 6 Aug 1681)

1681   ROBERT TANNER, mr of chors only, 1681 (lay cl, 1680→)

1681-1710 WILLIAM GREGGS, Xtmas 1681–death (b ?1652; singing-man, York, 1670→; mr of chors, York, 1677-81; ?mr of chors only, Durham, ?late 1681; *bur* 16 Oct 1710)

1711-63   JAMES HESLETINE, 25 Mar 1711–death (b ?1692; chor, Chapel Royal, ←1707; d 20 Jun 1763)

1763-1811 THOMAS EBDON, sworn 1 Oct 1763–d 23 Sep 1811 (*bap* 30 Jul 1738; chor, 1748–lay cl; lay cl, 1756-64; George Chrishop covered to an unknown extent 1796-1803)

---

[58]   It is not known whether he was ever restored.

1811-13 CHARLES E. J. CLARKE, sworn 20 Nov 1811–Nov 1813 (*b* 19 Dec 1795; chor, Worcester, 1804→; app org, Worcester, 19 Nov 1813; *d* 28 Apr 1844)

1814-62 WILLIAM HENSHAW, MusD, 1 Jan 1814–31 Dec 1862 (*b* 1792; *d* 30 Oct 1877)

1863-1907 PHILIP ARMES, MA, MusD, app 20 Nov 1862, early 1863– ret 13 May 1907 (*b* 15 Aug 1836; chor, Norwich, 1846-8, and Rochester, 1848-50; New Coll., Oxford; org, Chichester, 1861-3; 1st Prof. of Music, Durham Univ., 1897; *d* 10 Feb 1908)

1907-32 Revd ARNOLD D. CULLEY, MA, MusB, ?Sep 1907–ret Nov 1932) *b* 9 Mar 1867; org scholar, Emmanuel Coll, Camb, 1891; ordained, 1894; min can and prec, Durham, 1906; *d* 3 Dec 1947)

1933-36 JOHN DYKES BOWER, MA, DMus, Apr 1933–Oct 1936 (*b* 13 Aug 1905; Corpus Christi Coll, Camb; org & mr of chors, Truro, 1926-9; org, New Coll, Oxford, 1929-33; org, St Paul's, London, 1936-67; CVO, 1953; Kt, 1968; *d* 29 May 1981)

1936-74 CONRAD W. EDEN, DMus (Hon), Nov 1936–ret May 1974 (*b* 4 May 1905; chor, Wells; org exhibitioner, St John's Coll, Oxf, 1924-7; org, Wells, 1933-6; *d* 16 Oct 1994) (Alan Thurlow, sub-org, deputized during inter-regnum)

[1939-45 CYRIL B. MAUDE, FRCO, ARCM, sub-org, Sep 1939–Aug 1945, when org away on military service) (*b* ?1892; assist org, Durham, except for above period, May 1919–30 Apr 1967; *d* 1 May 1968)]

1974-85 RICHARD H. LLOYD, MA, Hon FGCM, Sep 1974–resig 31 Aug 1985 (*b* 25 Jun 1933; chor, Lichfield, 1942-7; org scholar, Jesus Coll, Camb, 1952-5; assist org, Salisbury, 1957-66; org, Hereford, 1966-74; dep head, Salisbury cathedral sch, 1985-8)

1985- JAMES B. LANCELOT, MusB, MA, Hon FRSCM, Hon FGCM, Oct 1985→ (*b* 2 Dec 1952; chor, St Paul's, London, 1961-6; org scholar, King's Coll, Camb, 1971-4; sub-org, Winchester, 1975-85; lay canon, Durham, 2002)

Masters and Headmasters

1820-64   THOMAS BROWN, app 9 Dec 1820–resig 13 Feb 1864 (chor, 1805-14; superintend of boys, 1814-17; supernum lay cl, 1813→; lay cl, 1819-62; *d* 20 May 1864)

1864-5   DAVID LAMBERT, app 13 Feb 1864–services dispensed with, Xtmas 1865 (supernum chor, 1845-8; lay cl, 1863–death during Evensong, 30 Oct 1873)

1865-6   RICHARD LAWSON, app 30 Dec 1865–death, 26 Oct 1866 (*b* 16 July 1843; Diocesan Training Sch, 29 Jan 1862; mr at Blue Coat Sch, Durham, 1865)

1866-71   JOSEPH LAWSON, app 20 Nov 1866–resig *c*.June 1871 to become ordained (*b* 29 Aug 1835; Dioc. Tr. Sch., 19 Jan 1854; mr at St Oswald's Sch, Durham, Jun 1866; *d* 10 Dec 1903)

1871-6   THOMAS LAWSON, *c*.Jun 1871–resig 30 Jun 1876 to become ordained (*b* 12 Apr 1846; Dioc. Tr. Sch, 30 Jan 1865; *d* 25 Feb 1899)

1876-1901   HENRY P. MEADEN, Jul 1876–ret *c*.Aug 1901 (*b* 1835; Chester Coll; F.C.S., 1863; headmaster, Ballymena Classical and Mercantile Sch, late 1860s→; mr at St Oswald's Parish Schs, ←1872-76; *d* 30 Jun 1907)

1901-14   Revd ARTHUR R. DOLPHIN, MA, Sep 1901–resig 14 Feb 1914, for living of Edmundbyers (*b* 29 Oct 1875; Oriel Coll, Oxf; sworn min can, Durham, 1 Jun 1901; *d* 19 Dec 1957)

1914-29   Revd FREDERICK S. DENNETT, MA, app 7 Feb 1914, commenced 15 Apr 1914–resig 5 Jan 1929 (but helped until Jul 1929), for living of Shincliffe (Peterhouse, Camb; min can, *c*.Feb 1914; *d* 18 Feb 1947)

[1929   TOM BARTON, 'acting-Headmaster', Jan–Aug 1929 (*b* 1891; assist mr, 1919–*d* 15 Mar 1950)]

1929-57   Revd HENRY Y. GANDERTON, MA, Sep 1929–ret 31 Aug 1957 (*b* 30 May 1893; St John's Coll, Durham; vice-prin there, 1924-9; min can, 1929-32 and 1933-47; hon can, 1947; *d* 9 Oct 1975)

1957-78   Revd JOHN M. GROVE, MA, 1 Sep 1957–ret 31 Aug 1978 (*b* 31 Oct 1913; Exhib. Magdalene Coll, Camb; chaplain, Dover Coll., 1940-3; chaplain, Clifton Coll, Bristol, 1943-57; hon can, 1974; *d* 14 Jul 2001)

1978-94   RAYMOND G. LAWRENCE, MA, 1 Sep 1978–ret 30 Apr 1994 (*b* 6 Feb 1930; Royal Navy Seaman Officer, Jan 1948–Oct 1970, ret in rank of Commander; Clare Coll, Camb, 1970-3; Taunton Sch, 1973-8)

1994-2002   C. STEPHEN S. DREW, MA, 1 Apr 1994 – 31 Aug 2002 (*b* 16 Nov 1950; chor, King's Coll, Camb; Exhibitioner, Lincoln Coll, Oxford; assistant teacher, Eton College, 1972-84; Head of English, Rugby Sch, 1984-8; house-master, Rugby Sch, 1988-94; Headmaster, St Faith's School, Cambridge, 2002 →)

2002→   IAN T. A. HAWKSBY, BA, 1 Sep 2002→ (b 23 Jan 1960; Leeds University; Manchester University PGCE Primary; LEA Primary teacher; Headmaster, Holy Trinity C of E [Aided] Primary School, Seaton Carew, Jan 1998-2002)